ETHNICITY, GENDER AND THE SUBVERSION OF NATIONALISM

D1526178

Ethnicity, Gender and the Subversion of Nationalism

edited by

FIONA WILSON
and
BODIL FOLKE FREDERIKSEN

FRANK CASS • LONDON

in association with

EADI The European Association of Development Research
and Training Institutes (EADI), Geneva

First Published 1995 in Great Britain by
FRANK CASS AND COMPANY LIMITED
Newbury House, 900 Eastern Avenue
London IG2 7HH

and in the United States of America by
FRANK CASS
c/o ISBS
5804 N.E. Hassalo Street, Portland, Oregon 97213-3644

Copyright © 1995 Frank Cass & Co. Ltd.

British Library Cataloguing in Publication Data
A catalogue record for this book is available
from the British Library

ISBN 0 7146 4155 3 (pbk)

Library of Congress Cataloging-in-Publication Data

Ethnicity, gender, and the subversion of nationalism / edited by Fiona
    Wilson and Bodil Folke Frederiksen
        p. cm.
    Published also as v. 6, no. 2 of The European journal of
development research.
    Includes bibliographical references.
    ISBN 0-7146-4155-3 (pbk)
    1. Ethnicity – Developing countries. 2. Sex role – Developing
countries. 3. Nationalism – Developing countries. 4. Women in
development – Developing countries. 5. Women – Developing countries –
Social conditions. I. Wilson, Fiona. II. Frederiksen, Bodil
Folke, 1943-   .
GN495.6.E885   1995   94-43142
305.8–dc20   CIP

This group of studies first appeared in a Special Issue on 'Ethnicity, Gender and the
Subversion of Nationalism' of the *European Journal of Development Research*, Vol.6.,
No.2, December 1994 published by Frank Cass & Co. Ltd.

Typeset by Frank Cass, London

Contents

Introduction:
Ethnicity, Gender and the Subversion of Nationalism

FIONA WILSON and BODIL FOLKE FREDERIKSEN

THE POLITICS OF IDENTITY

The politics of identity have come to stay. For a long time social groups have made their choices and organised their lives according to dimensions of identity. In the social sciences the division of labour within academic disciplines and shifting fashions have meant that this fact has been taken up and discussed only sporadically. Anthropology, political science, and social psychology debated and researched questions of identity in the 1950s and 1960s, women's studies have been engaged with male and female identities since the 1970s, and, interestingly, the recent agenda-setting academic work on identities has been spearheaded by departments of literature, particularly in the United States.

In its short career development studies has tended to consider 'identity' whether based on gender, religion, or ethnicity to be an obstacle to development, in so far as the discipline has pondered the subject at all. The uncritical use in development studies and development practice of concepts such as 'grass roots' and 'participation' indicates a wilful denial of the relevance of identity-based social difference and inequality in Third World societies.

On the other hand, questions of social collectivity and political identity have for a long time been central for those policy-makers who are accountable to nation state or local government authorities rather than to free-floating development bureaucracies. Hegemonic control by state or local authorities presupposes that the people concerned are willing to define themselves and form groups and organisations along lines of similarities often imposed from above. This is true in a colonial situation and in a complex developing society. If people do not willingly form allegiances, a great deal of violence must be expended to secure domination. Historically identities have been created in a tension between policy-oriented definitions from the outside and self-

Fiona Wilson, Centre for Development Research, Copenhagen, Denmark; Bodil Folke Frederiksen, International Development Studies, Roskilde University Centre, Denmark.

ᴜᴄɪinitions. They fluctuate in accordance with local, national and global power politics; they are pragmatic and contested.

Identities spring from people's core experience. But not from any essence. They are constructed in a strategic field with an eye to maximising possibilities of choice. They are informed by people's perspectives and knowledge of a narrow or broader locality. The knowledge which goes into a self-defined identity is privileged. Nobody is a greater expert than yourself. You are master of your own identity. Not in the sense that it is not contested, it probably is, because there may be no space for your particular identity in a world of scarce resources. But it is privileged in the sense that you are at home in it. It is familiar; your knowledge of it has no rival. In that sense identity is the ultimate popular knowledge.

Conflicts over definitions of identity are often violent. At the personal level this stems from the hurt felt when an outsider has the power to define identity in ways which deny the individual's own expert knowledge, composed as it is of core experiences, desires and yearnings and strategic plans for life. Utopian ideas are often powerful elements in the construction, or perhaps rather the imagining of identities. They represent the reverse side of dystopian realities and may be clung to with a passion which is proportional to the distance between the experienced reality and the desired ideal. Similar points may be raised with regards to claims to a shared ethnicity.

RELATING ETHNIC AND GENDER IDENTITIES

Ethnicity has stood for a group's way of conceptualising and relating to the enveloping society. In some cases, ethnicity may be mobilised to be constitutive of the concept of a nation [*Smith, 1991*]. The concept welds together individuals who share history, culture and community; who have an amalgam of language, religion, and regional belonging in common; and, perhaps most critical of all, feel they come from the same stock. Somewhere, far back, they have been a kin group, clan or tribe. And as emphasised in anthropological debates about ethnicity in the 1960s, one can often understand more by focusing on the boundary of an ethnic group rather than on 'the cultural stuff that it encloses' [*Barth, 1969: 15*]. Most earlier discussions of ethnicity failed to explore questions of gender or the implications that follow when the imagery of genealogy, kin and clan lie at the root of ethnic identities. Useful recent literature discussing relations between gender, ethnicity and nationalism include Davin [*1978*], Yuval-Davis and Anthias [*1989*], Anthias and Yuval-Davis [*1992*], and Brah [*1993*].

Given the underlying idiom of kinship, it has been hard for ethnicity to escape from racist overtones. If group membership is perceived of as something passed on by parents to children, as a kind of birthright, then we find comparable notions to the ideology of 'purity of blood' which, as Stolcke discusses in her contribution, underlay the socio-racial hierarchies of colonial South America. Where ideas of heritage and inheritance become intermingled in this way, issues surrounding the reproduction of the group become centrally important.

One major field in which gender intersects with ethnicity is thus social reproduction and the way that the ethnic line is carried on. Women are bearers not just of children in the abstract, but of children who will grow up to be members of the ethnic group. So it is through controlling women that ethnic boundaries can be kept in place and over time demarcate the juncture between internal cohesion and external difference. This carries critical implications for marriage patterns and the ways women's reproductive capacities are commandeered and controlled by the social group. Where concepts of heredity and purity of blood underpin identities, 'concerns about "racial contamination" may stir patriarchal fears about women's sexuality' [Brah, 1993]. In such societies, rape is no longer an individual criminal act but becomes a crime against an entire people. Systematic rape has been used throughout history as a deliberate strategy to defile and subjugate particular peoples, as Stolcke reminds us in the case of Latin America, and which we continue to witness whether in Vietnam or former Yugoslavia.

Although ethnic groups stress social reproduction and the concern to carry on the ethnic line, this does not mean that identities and relations of either gender or ethnicity are immutable or the same cross-culturally. The major ruptures and social transformations marked by conquest and colonisation, by the struggle for independence and institution of nation states, by the active formulation of discourses and policies of nationalism and modernisation, have led states and local populations to recode and re-elaborate gender identities and relations as well as alter the meanings and understandings given to race and ethnicity (as Wilson explores with respect to post-colonial Peru).

It is important, to avoid forms of analysis that assume stasis or permanence, even when looking at social relations of reproduction that tend, cross-culturally, to be notoriously enduring. Gender subordination, like ethnic oppression, is resisted and contested, though perhaps not openly and not all the time. Lived experiences of one form of oppression can generate a greater understanding of other dimensions of social inequality. This, Webster argues, has happened in the case of groups of 'tribal' women in India as a result of the experiences and hardships of labour migration.

A second important intersection of gender and ethnicity can be found in the ideologies, stereotypes and practices employed to underline the specificity of an ethnic group, signal its superiority and offer legitimation for political action. Ideas of shared ethnicity mean that members of a group take pains to signal through appearance and conduct their closeness to one another while at the same time stressing their difference from others. The codes of appearance and conduct often take explicitly gendered forms, with women possibly charged more than men with upholding a group's culture and identity. Gender stereotyping, when interwoven with ethnic identity, can give ample scope for chauvinism. 'Our women/men are circumcised, dress modestly, are chaste, behave with propriety and are thus of higher moral value and worth', and so on. It is not so much the registering of cultural difference that is at stake, rather the tendency for cultural claims to be embedded in claims of superiority and/or incompatibility with respect to others. The tendency for colonialists to fashion their own superiority as a contrast to the imputed immorality of the colonised, especially of the native women, has long been a feature of the colonial encounter.

Lonsdale [1992], in his interpretation of Kikuyu history, has drawn a useful distinction between political tribalism that is directed from above with the active collaboration of groups who see an advantage in defining themselves as such in certain historical conjunctures and moral ethnicity which has grown out of the lived and known experiences of a particular community. Yet the tenacity and responses to claims of ethnicity vary very considerably. Uprooting and urbanisation can mean that ethnic identities and stereotypes lose their bite, as Tranberg Hansen concludes from her studies of poor urban neighbourhoods in Lusaka, Zambia. In contrast, Frederiksen argues with respect to popular culture in Kenya that it would be rash to conclude, on the basis of the overwhelming presentation of gender and absence of explicit treatments of African ethnic difference in popular writing, that the former is considered more politically or socially relevant than the latter.

Ethnicity has been described as the politicisation of culture. Under its banner people seek to defend and promote their own culture in opposition to others. The aim may be to get more attention from a state, may be to bring it down or take it over, may be to work from within to question, undermine, or subvert it. But no conclusions can be drawn a priori about relations of power. Ethnicity demarcates a domain where power may be relatively diffuse or relatively concentrated; where it may be the preserve of men or shared with women. Since the internal power relations are so nebulous, there is ample space for them not only to be re-created but also become hijacked to suit contemporary needs or specific political purposes.

In the present day, ethnicity's most salient feature from a political perspective is that it seeks to link images of a distant past with the present and by so doing, construct a culturally-informed vantage point from which to report on and respond to contemporary situations of impoverishment and powerlessness. This will have an important bearing on the way political action is conducted and legitimated. But no hard or fast generalisations can be made with respect to gender or to the autonomy or authority granted women.

Recalling an ethnic past may build on images of a bygone patriarchal order or on visions of gender complementarity and harmony. Thus understandings of masculinity and femininity, as well as concern over their apparent erosion and loss, can underpin the ways ethnic identity is being currently re-worked and re-constituted (as discussed by Raikes in the case of Kisii identity). In the over-populated Kisii district of Kenya there has been no space for the unfolding of masculinity. The result is that discourses springing from different identities, such as youth or femininity, mingle with and may subvert the historically dominant discourses. Social groups who find themselves in the midst of chang-ing, contested identities are far more open to the ethnic and political definitions being suggested or imposed from the outside and more vulnerable to becom-ing incorporated in the power play of others, as Kaarsholm argues in the case of the Zulu Inkatha movement in South Africa.

A third area of discussion where gender and ethnicity intersect concerns the rise and decomposition of nationalism. How ethnicity is mobilised to generate nationalism needs to be discussed empirically. In some parts of the world, nationalism can be prefigured in widely-shared social memories of culturally and ethnically relatively homogeneous groups but in former colonial countries, nationalist struggles for independence have often demanded the construction of a sense of nation amongst peoples who felt themselves ethnically to be very different. The rise of nationalist ideologies can be associated with conser-vatism, especially with respect to the position of women. Although women have been in the forefront of the struggles against colonialism and racism, sub-sequent nationalist discourse has tended to remove women from the public arena and emphasise an ideal of women's domesticity (as Wilson notes in the case of nineteenth-century Peru). Though nationalist movements may seek to incorporate women, ways are found to limit and control the kind of emancipa-tion that is offered as Hansen discusses in the case of a Hindu nationalist movement in India.

But the cultural underpinnings of nationalism, along with the particular ideological insistence on the cultural homogeneity of the nation, have been changing shape. As a consequence, the meanings given to ethnicity and gender undergo a sea change. In a transnational world, one can no longer make do with the old assumptions as to people's fundamental rootedness or preferred sedentariness. Local societies have been brought increasingly into contact with global events, culture and patterns of consumption; it is a creolising world. Not all, however, are empowered or entitled physically to move. One terrible legacy of nationalism has been the harassment and displacement of population groups described as unfit for nationalist dreams of modernity and sovereignty. Refugees are stuck in a no-man's land of camps.

Borders are contested and more permeable (at least when it comes to illicit movement) than many believe. People find ways of crossing borders in their search for new livelihoods and/or greater personal security. More than ever before, it is women who are both transnational migrants and refugees. Both refugee and migrant groups are pressed into questioning and reconstructing their understandings of gender, ethnicity and class in order to respond actively to the new situations of multi-locality as Nyberg Sørensen discusses with respect to the constant movement of people between the Dominican Republic and New York.

The studies in this collection are experimental. The contributors have been concerned to problematise the relations between race, ethnicity and gender. Each author attempts to explore and elucidate different aspects of the relationship. Some of the contributors remain somewhat hesitant about their results while others describe enthusiastically the new perspectives opened up by their enquiries. The studies are not deeply theoretical. Instead most of the authors have chosen to take a fresh look at an existing body of case study material in order to enquire more deeply into relationships that were submerged or only glimpsed at in passing in previous analyses. As a result, one can say that the discussions are well and truly grounded. Our hope is that these case studies will prompt others to ask more questions and provoke fuller analyses and theorisations of what relations between ethnicity and gender entail.

REFERENCES

Anthias, F. and N. Yuval-Davis, 1992, *Racial Boundaries*, London: Routledge.
Barth, F., 1969, *Ethnic Groups and Boundaries*, London: George Allen & Unwin.
Brah, Avtar, 1993, 'Re-framing Europe: En-Gendered Racisms, Ethnicities and Nationalisms in Contemporary Western Europe', *Feminist Review*, No.45.
Davin, Anna, 1978, 'Imperialism and Motherhood', *History Workshop*, Issue 5.
Lonsdale, J. 1992, 'The Moral Economy of Mau Mau: Wealth, Poverty and Civic Virtue in Kikuyu Political Thought', in B. Berman and J. Lonsdale (eds.), *Unhappy Valley: Conflict in Kenya and Africa, Book II*, London: James Currey.
Smith, A. D., 1991, *National Identity*, Harmondsworth: Penguin.
Yuval-Davis, N. and F. Anthias, 1989, *Women-Nation-State*, Basingstoke: Macmillan.

Invaded Women: Sex, Race and Class in the Formation of Colonial Society

VERENA STOLCKE

Until recently, the history of the Conquest of the Americas was presented in such a way as to omit systematically questions of gender. Even the more critical accounts ignored the manner in which indigenous women (and later black women) had been forced to live through the assaults on their personal and cultural integrity. Little attempt was made to explore the consequences this had for the formation of colonial society. These consequences are the subject of this study.

Certain chronicles, such as Guaman Poma de Ayala's '*Nueva Crónica y Buen Gobierno*' did denounce the sexual abuse and other humiliations suffered by women. As in the case of all wars, indigenous women were part of the booty coveted by the Spanish conquerors. But rape was more than a matter of sexual enjoyment; taking women from the ranks of the defeated carried a deeper significance. It sealed definitively the total victory of the Spanish in that, according to their way of thinking, they were appropriating the most important possession of the defeated: their women.

Historians, however, have read the accounts in the chronicles in a highly selective way. The Conquest of the Americas has been narrated from a male perspective: it is represented as acts of aggression and dispossession carried out by a group of strong men, the Spanish, against a group of weak men, the 'Indians'. The historiography of the Conquest presents us with images of the victims, but these are stereotypes, far removed from reality.

One can quote the example of Garcilaso the Inca. He was the illegitimate son of a high–ranking Spanish official, a Corregidor, in Peru and an Inca princess and thus belonged to noble families on both sides. Although his Spanish father married a Spanish woman who was presumably of 'pure blood' instead of marrying his Inca mother, Garcilaso was recognised by his father and hence also by Spanish society. This was quite a common practice of the time and noted in historiography. Nevertheless, despite such recognition, he was never able to free himself completely from the stain of his illegitimate origins and was barred from inheriting his father's honours and titles.

Another highly emblematic case is that of Doña Marina, the Aztec woman

Verena Stolcke, Autonomous University of Barcelona, Spain. An earlier version of this contribution appeared in Margo Henrickes and Patricia Parker (eds.), *Women, 'Race', and Writing in the early Modern Period*, published by Routledge, London, 1994.

who became Cortes's interpreter and lover, popularly known as 'La Malinche' or 'La Chingada'. This last term is fraught with sexual meanings. It is still commonly used in Mexico to mean 'the violated' and it reflects an enormous ambivalence surrounding the image constructed of La Malinche. She is portrayed as both the victim of violation and as Cortes's consenting and useful instrument who enabled him to conquer Mexico. Cortes, who already had a Spanish wife, never married La Malinche. Instead, although he recognised his child by her, he forced her to marry a soldier from his entourage.

Octavio Paz describes her in *The Labyrinth of Solitude* as the quintessence of indigenous collaboration. Even up to the present day, the term '*malinchismo*' is still used in Mexico to mean betrayal of one's country. The ambiguous interpretation of Doña Marina is highly revealing in that it exonerates the conqueror and the violator while holding the victim responsible for her own misfortunes.

The reconstruction of pre-Colombian socio-political organisation as well as of relations rooted in gender is made particularly difficult on account of the cultural diversity of the conquered peoples and the disturbing effects of the Conquest. One faces enormous difficulties in trying to interpret available sources of information and assess their significance. There is no doubt, though, about certain issues. The Conquest brought devastating diseases, forced conversion to Christianity, the introduction of new crops and animals, new mining methods and an oppressive regime of labour coercion, and the imposition of the Spanish language. But one aspect of the Conquest that has been less well described is the sexual abuse and violence against indigenous women.

Through a critical reading of the chronicles, Irene Silverblatt [*1987*] has tried to correct this distorted, 'blind' view of the experiences of indigenous women in Peru. She shows how the violence of the Conquest dramatically upset the more complementary relations between women and men prevailing under the Inca Empire. In the early years of the Spanish colony, the noble Inca lineages were considered to possess a social status similar to that of the Spanish nobility; thus Inca women were partly protected on account of their noble birth. However, even women of rank, whom the conquerors made their legitimate wives, came to lose much of their previous autonomy.

For the vast majority of indigenous women, the Conquest meant the loss of material, political and ritual privileges; exploitation of their labour; and sexual abuse by the invading soldiers and priests who crucified them in bed under the pretext of saving their souls. Many cases of 'solicitation' were brought against members of the clergy who had sexually assaulted indigenous women. 'Solicitation' was recognised as a crime and brought before the Inquisition.

The invaded women had always resisted the attacks made on them but the Spanish succeeded in transforming what had been strongly complementary relationships between women and men into relationships of domination.

Indigenous women suffered for the first time material, cultural, spiritual and sexual oppression.

IDEOLOGICAL DIMENSIONS OF CONQUEST

I wish to turn now to discussing the more ideological dimensions of the Conquest and to analysing ways in which conceptualisations of society and race brought from Europe were diffused by colonial elites in the Americas. This was a new society under formation and it is important to show how the imported ideas were reformulated and adapted so as to suit quite different local circumstances in order to legitimise and perpetuate the new social hierarchic order. I want to argue that the formation of this colonial society came to affect women in very specific ways.

Little attention has yet been paid to the dialectical interplay between the culture brought from the metropolis by the conquerors and the ideological organising principles through which that culture was implanted in the colonies and which moulded the trajectory of colonial society for centuries to come. This is quite a different theme from an analysis of European fantasies about 'savage man' that were typical in the period.

Up to now, historical accounts of colonial society have tended to fall into two categories. Some have tried to excuse and justify the Conquest on the grounds of its civilising mission. Other more critical accounts have denounced the underlying political economy of colonisation and imperialist exploitation of new territories, arguing that this led to a wholesale imposition of spiritual, social and political values on an autochthonous population. But to date, no detailed studies have explored what happened at the cultural interface or have shown how and why particular cultural values were selected and transformed in the process of colonisation.

Miscegenation or '*mestizaje*' was one immediate consequence of the Conquest. The sexual rapacity of the conquerors and widespread concubinage led to the birth of increasing numbers of mestizos. From the earliest days of the colony, mestizos were considered socially inferior and were discriminated against. This was partly because the new population group presented a challenge to the structure of colonial society.

Perceived differences are always constructed historically. The Conquest, whose objective was the domination and exploitation of the local population, gave rise to a profoundly unequal society. This inequality could have been conceptualised and legitimised in various ways. There was no pre-ordained way; it might have been possible, for example, to have adopted meritocratic principles, but the Conquest did not occur in an ideological vacuum. On the contrary the Crown, the Church, the conquerors, the secular and religious authorities, all possessed (apart from greed) a vision of the world founded on a project of colonisation and exploitation. This shared vision overrode internal differences and diversity of individual interests. Clearly, there was an ideological struggle under way, concerning not only the status and treatment of indigenous peoples but also the question of whether they could be defined as human beings. If they were human, and thus essentially equal to the Spanish, they were capable of conversion to Christianity. If they were defined as 'naturally' different and inferior, then criteria were needed with which to justify and perpetuate this inferiority.

Differences of culture and phenotype in the Americas came to acquire profound political and social significance. This was inspired by contemporary European ideas about social inequalities and the institutional mechanisms and procedures required to perpetuate them. Even though metropolitan ideas about social classification and segregation were not necessarily appropriate to the new colonial socio-political reality, they were part of the cultural and ideological burden transported by the Spanish to the so-called New World, and they played a decisive role in constructing the socio-economic and political inequalities of colonial society.

Doctrine of 'Purity of Blood'

I want to analyse in greater depth here the metropolitan doctrine based on *limpieza de sangre* (purity of blood) and the conceptualisations of marriage and legitimacy that it inspired which came to acquire new meanings of transcendental importance for women in the American colonies. I want to elucidate in the case of colonial society what an English doctor cryptically wrote in the mid-nineteenth century: 'the uterus is to the Race what the heart is to the person: it is the organ of circulation for the species' [*Poovey, 1987: 145*].

Modern racism can be taken to mean the attribution of socio-economic inequalities and exclusions to alleged racial, and hence hereditary deficiencies. Frequently racism has been interpreted as a perverse consequence of European imperial expansion dating from the nineteenth century. But this is to misunderstand the roots of racist ways of thinking. Racist ideological constructs were already present in Europe by the fifthteenth century, and were to hand to justify colonisation and to shape colonial society.

The origins and etymological history of the word *raza* (race) are polemical. Fragmentary evidence exists as to the use of the word *raza* in Spanish, *raça* in Portuguese and *race* in French from the thirteenth century, though it is only in the sixteenth century that the terms appear in frequent use. However, the connotations of the term appear to have diverged significantly, depending on their political and geographical context. According to some authors, the French term *race* initially implied membership and descent of a family, or a (house) in the positive sense of a 'noble lineage'. *Stirpis nobilita* [*1512*] is translated, for example, as *noblesse de sang* (noble blood) in 1533. But this meaning of race is first cited lexigraphically in the 19th century: 'il vient d'une noble race'.

The Spanish term *raza* was used to mean the succession of generations: *de raza en raza* as well as the members of a given generation. Through this kind of usage, a close connection was established between ideas of 'nobility' and 'quality'. Stemming from its connection with the image of an inherited community, the term 'race' is vested with political and social significance. It is this particular etymological origin that was selected by the German author, Conze [*1984: 135–78*]. Corominas [*1982*], on the other hand, explains the term using other linguistic roots. By the mid–fifteenth century, race had taken on connotations coming from an apparently similar word, *raca*, meaning flaw, defect or fault (as in woven cloth). From the sixteenth century, the term appeared in Castilian Spanish in relation to the idea of purity of blood and it acquired a pejorative meaning. Thus although the Castilian definition of *raza* appears to have multiple etymological roots, Corominas concludes that 'when the foreign term "raza" in the biological sense of having to do with the species, penetrated into Castilian, it was natural for the word to be contaminated with this pejorative tinge, especially when applied to Moors and Jews', though the precise negative connotations were not constant [*Corominas, 1982: 800–801*].

Clearly, the meanings given to the word 'race' were never neutral. And the etymological and political differences embedded in the term *raza* are of particular relevance for the arguments of this analysis. The criterion of 'race' was being adopted in the metropolis as a way of legitimating the discrimination and persecution of non-Christian communities. At a later date, it also came to be used to discriminate against the descendants of non-Christians, who had by then been converted to Christianity. In other words, faith came to be seen as something inherited.

The Conquest of the Americas coincided with a period in Spanish history known as the *Reconquista*. This started with the politically and ideologically motivated expulsion or compulsory conversion of the Jews in 1492. A century later (1609–14) converted Moslems or *Moriscos* as they were known, were also expelled from Spain. In the mid-fifteenth century, the Council of Toledo adopted the first statute concerning *limpieza de sangre* (purity of blood). Four years after the Spanish Inquisition was founded in 1480, it was decreed in its constitution that those sentenced for offences against the Christian faith would be barred from holding public office. Towards the end of the fifthteenth century various statutes referring to purity of blood were adopted by religious and military orders, universities and halls of residence, as well as by some municipal bodies and cathedrals in Spain. This inspired certain private societies to adopt similar statutes, even though they never formed part of Spanish Imperial laws.

The Inquisition was the sole tribunal which had jurisdiction over the issue of purity of blood. The *Santo Oficio* (Holy Office), as the ecclesiastical tribunal was called, was set up to prosecute crimes against Christianity, principally Judaism and Mohammedism, and this body became the mediator between theories of exclusion and the constitution of society. The Tribunal embodied the view that all converted to Christianity could still be potential heretics [*Kamen, 1986*].

Even though Catholicism had begun as a universalistic religion, it came to exclude non-believers from social honour. Initially there had been a loophole: the possibility of religious conversion. Through baptism, Jews and Moslems had the chance to become like gentiles. In other words, religious faith had not yet been considered an original attribute but was something that could be freely acquired so long as the conversion was sincere. But towards the middle of the fifthteenth century what had begun as religious-cultural discrimination was transformed into racism, with the creation of racially antagonistic groups.

Racism provided the motives and the means by which to persecute and marginalise particular groups in society by declaring that their previous conversion was null and void. 'A racist doctrine of original sin of the most repulsive kind' was being introduced [*Kamen, 1985: 158*]. Although many people still believed that a baptised Jew should be treated in the same way as a baptised gentile (Diaz de Montalvo, cited by Kamen [*1985: 159*]), all converts to Christianity as well as all 'moriscos' became objects of suspicion and discrimination as a result of the doctrine of purity of blood.

Through this doctrine, 'true' Christians were considered to be families that were not racially mixed; and excluded from the 'true' faith were Moslems, Jews, heretics or *penitenciados*, that is those who had been condemned by the Inquisition. The doctrine underlined the belief that one could no longer choose to belong to a particular faith; belonging to a religion other than Christianity had been transformed into an inherent and inherited stain that was passed on through the 'blood' from generation to generation and in this way was indelible. As Henry Kamen [*1985: 158*] has pointed out: 'In the 15th century, many people felt that religious and national honour could only be preserved by assuring the purity of the lineage and by avoiding the mixture of Jewish or Moslem blood'.

Once religion was transformed into a natural and hereditary attribute, the zeal of those charged with safeguarding the religious-racial hierarchy established a close connection between purity of blood, endogamous marriage and (as proof of the former) legitimate birth. The Inquisition undertook to examine genealogies in order to prevent false declarations of purity, so it also played a part in shoring up these notions.

The statutes relating to purity of blood sought to exclude all those who could not demonstrate their purity from qualifying for offices of trust and from social pre-eminence. However, putting such statutes into effect was by no means unproblematic. To the consternation of the Spanish nobility, who for centuries had happily brought Jews and Moslems into their families, the only authentic Christians of ancient stock were found to be the plebians. In the face of this paradox of classification, disputes intensified within the elite itself and cases concerning the religious-racial doctrine were increasingly taken to the Inquisition [*Kamen, 1986*]. While, on the one hand, opposition grew as to how lawyers and theologians could apply the doctrine, on the other, the concept of purity was gradually extended to cover other 'stains' such as social class. Questions were raised, for example, as to how servile occupations could be fitted in to the racial doctrine underlying the socio-economic hierarchy.

The doctrine of purity of blood lost ground in Spain by the late eighteenth century and the Holy Office of the Inquisition was abolished in the early nineteenth century. A little later, earlier stipulations regarding the taking of blood tests prior to marriage were also abolished. Thus it is possible to show that the idea that some people were more equal than others before God on account of their racial origins was a belief fashioned in Europe initially for domestic use. In colonial society, the evolution of the concept of purity of blood took a different course. Moors, Jews and their children; gypsies; anyone not reconciled to the Church; and the children and grandchildren of all those publically condemned by the Inquisition; as well as the children and grandchildren of all those burnt at the stake or condemned for heresy or apostasy whether through the masculine or feminine line were denied passage to 'the Indies' [*Martínez, 1983*]. But it does not, of course, follow that members of these groups never reached the Americas. This is but one example of the many ways that the concept of purity of blood was extended to include new social groups.

By the sixteenth century in the colonial world, it was not always possible to distinguish mestizos from the 'pure'-blooded Spanish. Progressively, mestizos and mulattos faced greater discrimination and were disqualified and barred from entering the clergy or from holding public office [*Méchoulan, 1981: 58*]. In 1679, for example, the founding constitution of a seminary in Mexico stated that only boys who were 'clean and of pure blood, who were not of the Moorish race, were Jews or were condemned by the Holy Office, who had not recently converted to the faith, who were not mestizos, or mulatos...' would be admitted [*Konetzke, 1958–62, I: 691–2*].

The dramatic demographic decline of the indigenous population was an early consequence of the Conquest. A long debate then ensued between the Church and the colonial bureauracy on the situation and status of the survivors. For a time, serious suggestions were made that the indigenous peoples were descendants of the lost tribes of Israel, but eventually the Crown was forced to concede that they were pure of blood, except in those cases where conversion to the Christian faith was refused [*Méchoulan, 1981: 57*].

Racial Categorisation

The sixteenth and seventeenth centuries saw an increased migration from Europe to the Americas, as well as the transportation of many more African slaves to the 'New World'. Under the changing demographic conditions, the 'danger' of miscegenation was considered to be increasing. Reflecting this, the colonial social hierarchy was no longer founded on religious criteria but became explicitly based on race. Racial categorisations became ever more scrupulous and convoluted. Combined in one main racial category were free and enslaved blacks and various mixtures – *mulatos* and *zambos* (part African, part indigenous), *zamaigos* (part African, part Asian); in another category were Indians, (some of whom were *originarios* with full rights in their communities, while others were *forasteros* with more limited rights) and mestizos; and in a third category were the whites, both *peninsulares* (born in Spain) and *criollos* (born in the Americas), whether rich or poor.

The mulatto, mestizo and other racially mixed categories were particularly distrusted and disdained. Their existence made racial boundaries less certain, placed doubts on the underlying racial conceptualisations and actively threatened the emerging racial hierarchy. Towards the end of the seventeenth century, royal decrees multiplied in an attempt to clear up the many doubts about purity of blood and to grant dispensations so that some could enter the clergy or occupy official posts. This activity tended to reconfirm racial categories and legitimise the grounds for discrimination.

By the eighteenth century, the indigenous population was recovering for reasons that are still unclear, and the white population also continued to grow [*Sánchez Albornoz, 1984*]. The result was a further expansion of the mestizo and mulatto groups given that many white men chose to live with indigenous or negro women.

The growth of a racially mixed mestizo population has often been linked to the sexual excesses of the conquerors and their desire to make indigenous women, and later African women, their concubines. This behaviour by men has often been excused on the grounds of their emotional and sexual deprivation in a colonial society where few Spanish (that is marriageable) women were available. But the reality was probably quite different. The Crown had promulgated a profusion of decrees and laws demanding that those colonists who had wives in Spain must bring them across. The laws remained in force up to the eighteenth century. And it appears that by the mid-sixteenth century, there was no longer any real scarcity of Spanish women in the colonies, one indication of this being the foundation of the first convents to house the legitimate or natural daughters of the Spanish population when they failed to find marriage partners [*Konetzke, 1958–62, I: 691–2*].

The extent of concubinage shows that we are dealing with yet another manifestation of the power of the Spanish colonisers, who saw indigenous and African women as easy prey for sexual gratification. But it was more than this. At issue was a population and colonisation policy which was trying to safeguard the stability and security of the white colonies [*Konetzke, 1958–62, I: 148*]. It had not been easy to implement this policy. Cortes himself had shown characteristic duplicity. While he made risky incursions into unknown territories in the company of Doña Marina, he stipulated that: 'so as to make clear that the settlers of these regions intend to reside and remain in them, it is decreed that all persons holding Indians or married in Castile or elsewhere send for their wives within one and a half years...on pain of losing their Indians and all else they have won or acquired' [*Konetzke, 1958–62, I: 128*].

Colonial society had been converted into a multi-coloured human mosaic, full of complex inequalities as a result of the interaction between the criteria of class and race. Some benefited greatly (the white *peninsulares* and *criollos*) to the detriment of everyone else. The concept of purity of blood was not only reinforced, it also lost any remaining religious connotation and was transformed into a purely racist notion. The Crown was still insisting in 1734 that the *caciques* (leaders) and their descendants should retain all the distinctions and honours (in ecclesiastical and secular life) that were accorded to noble Castilians and that 'illustrious Indians and their descendants, who are of pure blood without mixture or of a condemned sect, retain all the prerogatives, distinctions and honours enjoyed by those of pure blood in the Realm' [*Konetzke, 1958–62, III: 217*]. Formally, then, during the Colony, the indigenous population still enjoyed certain privileges. In many cases, these privileges were only finally lost after Independence.

In spite of the racist structures set up, it is important to stress that colonial society never became a totally closed hierarchic order. On the contrary, the inherent contradictions threatened the social order in various ways. Sporadic sexual unions and concubinage were the essence of *mestizaje* [*Lavrín, 1989*]. Ironically, the mestizos who were the offspring of these extra-marital unions and who were considered racially inferior, were those best placed to undermine the hierarchy.

For the elites and their followers, legitimate birth and legitimate marriage acquired a new importance. Not only did legitimacy prove the moral decorum of their progenitors, but it also attested to their purity of blood, that is to say their race through inheritance. Illegitimate birth, on the other hand, was an indication of 'infamy, stain and defect' stemming from the mixture of races [*Konetzke, 1958–62, III: 473–4*]. Economic success could compensate up to a point for a lowly racial situation [*Martínez-Alier, 1974*] and the Spanish Crown could even grant dispensations of this 'stain'.

As colonial society became more complex, there were far greater possibilities for contact between the socio-racial categories and racism intensified.

The relative fluidity of the colonial order served to entrench still further the elite's obsession with racial purity. By basing social prestige on racial purity, the latter was only guaranteed by marriage between racial equals.

Doctrine of Spiritual Equality

Paradoxically, the Church's policy on marriage served to sharpen this tension. The Church opposed the secular hierarchy based on race and stressed instead a doctrine of spiritual equality. Until the eighteenth century, the Church held exclusive prerogative to perform the act of marriage. The doctrinal principle which determined ecclesiastical practice in this respect was freedom of marriage based on the consent of both parties. Canonical doctrine rejected the idea that parents had a right to interfere in the marriages of their children for reasons of social and/or racial inequality. Belonging to the same family whether through blood or proxy (that is through godparenthood) was the only important canonical impediment to marriage. Sexual virtue, that is to say virginity before marriage and chastity afterwards, was the highest mark of goodness in the eyes of the Church. Virtue should prevail, notwithstanding the caprices of society.

Already by the sixteenth century, there were cases of parents trying to stop their childrens' marriages for reasons of supposed social inequality (for Mexico, see Seed [1988]). In these disputes, the sexual virtue defended by the Church came up against the paternal concern to protect family purity and avoid the disgrace of an unsuitable marriage. The position of the Church in the colonies was enhanced when the Crown authorised the granting of greater powers to local ecclesiastical courts where matrimonial disputes were heard. The Church utilised the courts not only to defend the right of an individual to marry but also to combat the many practices of sexual irregularity. Sexuality should be confined to marriages realised between consenting parties, where procreation was the only goal. Canonical moral doctrine stressed sexual honour and ranked it higher than social prestige.

Given the attitude of the Church, the families of the elite had to struggle in other ways to avoid unsuitable unions. This was achieved largely by imposing strict control over women's sexuality. Protection signified control. In fact, the other side of the ecclesiastical policy of protecting moral virtue was sexual control. The salvation of the soul depended on the submission of the body, but in the colonies, the Church was never able to eradicate men's sexual exploitation of women outside of marriage in respect of women considered to come from inferior socio-racial backgrounds. Inter-racial unions not sanctified by the Church were mostly consensual, as they were euphemistically called at the time.

By exalting sexual virtue, the Church furthermore fomented discrimination between different categories of women, expressed in sexual terms. Women sexually abused by white men were considered promiscuous and were penalised because they were presumed to live in mortal sin while virtuous women, white women from respectable families, were subjected to a strict control of their sexuality.

The ecclesiastical authorities in the colonies certainly did not always uphold an egalitarian Christian morality. Doubts about this are raised by the sexual abuses so frequently committed by the clergy themselves. But the pre-nuptial disputes taken before the ecclesiastical court, such as when the Church insisted on marriage if a woman had been seduced after promise of marriage, or when a marriage was celebrated between social unequals, indicate that the Church did threaten the material interests of the elites. Attempts made by parents to impede unsuitable marriages reveal a profound conflict between the Church's aim of saving souls by preventing people from living in sin and the efforts of elites to preserve purity of blood as a basis for their social pre-eminence.

By the eighteenth century, the Church encountered increasing difficulties in its defence of the doctrine of freedom of marriage as against pre-nuptial interference by families. The Church's loss of jurisdiction over marriage has been explained by the way its defence of sexual and moral virtue was undermined by the growing obsession of the elite with socio-racial purity [*Seed, 1988*]. The Church was fighting on two fronts. On one side, the Spanish state was progressively limiting the power of the Church in various political arenas. On the other side, there was a growing conflict over which institution, the Church or the state, had ultimate jurisdiction in the cases of disputed marriages between socially unequal partners.

Secularisation of Marriage

In 1775 the Crown asked its Council of Ministers for a report on the provisions necessary in order to avoid marriages between unequals in view of 'the lamentable effects and serious damage caused by those marriages that are contracted between persons belonging to highly unequal circumstances and estates'. The Crown argued that

> the excessive favour extended by ecclesiastical ministers to the misconceived absolute freedom of marriage with no distinction made as to persons and, often carried out in opposition to the legitimate resistance by parents and relatives ... has been the main source from which has stemmed the major part of the damaging effects being suffered in Spain due to marriages between unequals [*Konetzke, 1958–62, III: 401–5*].

In 1776 Charles III promulgated the *Pragmática Sanción* in order to avoid the abuse of unequal marriages. Free choice in marriage was suppressed and marriages could only be performed if paternal consent was given, on pain of disinheritance. Some authors have interpreted the Pragmatic Sanction as a reaction by Charles III to the marriage of his younger brother to a woman of inferior social status [*Seed, 1988*]. It was promulgated at the time of the Bourbon reforms, in a period of intense political and social transformation. This was a time when ideas of individual liberty and equality were gaining ground in Europe and were also leaving their mark on Spain. In this more open socio-political climate, marriages between socially unequal parties were becoming much more frequent. At first sight, therefore, it appears paradoxical that, precisely at a time of political opening, liberalism and modernisation the Spanish Crown should introduce more severe controls with respect to marriage. The law, however, is not necessarily the juridical expression of changing social values, for frequently there exists instead a dialectical relationship between the law and society. Thus it is more plausible to interpret the Pragmatic Sanction as a last-ditch attempt at social control in a period when changing marriage practices seemed to threaten the established hierarchic order. It is by no means unusual for reformist states, lacking the strength to make a more thorough social transformation, to seek to use juridical means to control the possible social consequences.

Therefore in Spain, matrimonial regulations were being secularised and individual choice within marriage was being suppressed. This served to reinforce social hierarchy. This was also a period in which the doctrine of purity of blood was losing force. Matrimonial disputes were resolved henceforth in civil courts and various royal decrees were passed to reinforce paternal authority in matters of marriage. The situation was quite different in the colonies where, instead of disappearing, the doctrine of purity of blood experienced a belated renaissance.

In 1778 the Pragmatic Sanction was extended to the Indies

> bearing in mind that similar or more damaging effects are caused by this abuse (of marriage between social unequals) in my Realms and Dominions of the Indies due to their size and the diversity of classes and castes of their inhabitants ... and the serious harm which has been suffered due to the absolute and unregulated liberty of betrothals by the impassioned and incapable young of one or other sex [*Konetzke, 1958–62, III: 438–42*].

Excluded were 'the mulatos, negroes, coyotes, and individuals of similar castes and races known publically as such', who presumably possessed no honour that needed protection. In all other cases, paternal consent was demanded and only the civil authorities had the power to grant dispensation.

But the application of the Pragmatic Sanction in the colonies was beset by difficulties.

Those sections of society with limited material possessions had little to lose when marriages were contracted against the family's will. Although these marriages were infrequent, there were always individuals who wanted to marry for love or to regularise a sexual liaison in spite of social difference. Socio-racial prejudice and reasons of state did not succeed any more than the ecclesiastical moral imperatives had done.

I shall not analyse in detail the changing laws with respect to marriage as I have done this previously in the case of Cuba [*Martínez–Alier, 1974*]. Here I shall only highlight some of the repercussions resulting from the special characteristics of colonial society and the consequences these had for women.

After 1778 various additional royal decrees concerning unequal marriage were passed. These tended to make the situation regarding marriage more uncertain and unclear. In contrast to the civil authorities in the colonies, the Crown tended to give its support (allegedly for demographic reasons) to those wanting to marry even where there was paternal opposition. But a great degree of ambivalence prevailed with respect to interracial marriage. For their part, the colonial authorities demonstrated a renewed preoccupation with purity of blood, even though this doctrine was rapidly losing ground in the metropolis.

A decree passed in 1810 finally resolved the uncertainty. This stipulated that both the nobility and persons known to be pure in blood who had reached the age of majority had to obtain a licence from the colonial civil authorities if they wished to contract marriage with negroes, mulattos or members of other castes. This decree led to a virtual prohibition of all inter-racial marriages. It also showed clearly that matrimony was now a matter under the jurisdiction of the state. Not only were family interests at stake, but so also was the stability of the social order. In the colonies, social stability meant the preservation of racial hierarchy.

What consequences did this renewed emphasis on racism have for women? In all hierarchic societies, where social position is attributed to qualities that are supposedly inherent, natural, racial and therefore hereditary, it is absolutely essential for elites to control the procreative powers of their women in order to preserve their social pre-eminence. As a nineteenth century Spanish lawyer argued, only women could bring bastards into the family. In institutionalising the metaphysical notion of blood as a vehicle for family prestige and as an ideological instrument to guarantee social hierarchy, the state, in alliance with families pure in blood, subjected women to a more stringent control over their sexuality while their irresponsible sons were allowed to disport themselves with 'inferior' women who were regarded as being 'without quality'.

The Church had defended freedom of marriage so as to protect sexual virtue as a moral value in itself. The state converted women's sexual virtue into an instrument by which to protect the social body. This meant that some women, the daughters of white families, became tools, while other women, those considered 'without quality', became the victims of the socio-racial hierarchy. In a racist society, truly 'the uterus is for the Race what the heart is for the Individual'. But there is an important qualification. As noted already, we are not dealing with an unchanging or static social order. On the contrary, all the juridical paraphernalia regarding marriage was deemed necessary precisely because there were always women and men ready to reject the politico-racial order and the immoral values on which this rested.

In conclusion, it is important to stress once again that racism must not be thought of solely as the result of colonial expansion. The 'scientific' racism of the nineteenth century was constructed on the basis of earlier ideas about a metaphysical purity of blood. In its nineteenth century variant, racism also served to paper over the contradictions within societies where social classes were emerging and where a doctrine of individual merit clashed with an increasingly unequal social reality. Racism was a way out, a legitimation of renewed colonial expansion. However, racism and ethnic conflicts in contemporary Latin America cannot be reduced to a mere anachronistic residue left over from colonial times. On the contrary, they are rooted in the persisting social inequalities that prevail up to the present day. Latin America's socio-economic structure has changed in the past decades, mostly for the worse. With regard to the experience of women, those who are the daughters 'of family' have achieved some measure of freedom, but it is the vast numbers of poor women who bear the brunt of material hardship.

REFERENCES

Conze, Werner, 1984, 'Rasse', in Otto Brunner, Werner Conze and Reihnart Kosselleck (eds.), *Geschichtliche Grundbegriffe – Historisches Lexikon zur Politisch–Sozialen Sprache in Deutschland, Vol. 5*, Stuttgart: Ernest Klett.
Corominas, Joan, 1982, *Diccionario Crítico Etimológico Castellano e Hispánico*, Madrid: Editorial Gredos.
Kamen, Henry, 1985, *La Inquisición Española*, Barcelona: Crítica.
Kamen, Henry, 1986, 'Una Crisis de Conciencia en la Edad de Oro de España: Inquisición Contra la "Limpieza de Sangre"', *Bulletin Hispanique*, Vol.88, Nos.3–4.
Konetzke, Richard, 1958–62, *Colección de Documentos para la Historia de la Formación Social de Hispanoamérica, 1493–1810, Vols.I–III*, Madrid: Instituto Jaime Balmes, C.S.I.C.l.
Konetzke, Richard, 1945, 'La Emigración de Mujeres Españolas a América Durante la Época Colonial', *Revista Internacional de Sociología*, Jan./March, Vol.3, No.9.
Lavrín, Asunción (ed.), 1989, *Sexuality and Marriage in Colonial Latin America*, Lincoln, NE and London: University of Nebraska Press.
Martínez, José Luis, 1983, *Pasaieros de Indias*, Madrid: Alianza Editorial.
Martínez-Alier, Verena, 1974, *Marriage, Class and Colour in Nineteenth Century Cuba: A Study of Racial Attitudes and Sexual Values in a Slave Society*, Cambridge: Cambridge University Press.
Méchoulan, Henry, 1981, *El Honor de Dios*, Barcelona: Editorial Argos Vegara.
Poovey, Mary, 1987, 'Scenes of an Indelicate Character: The Medical Treatment of Victorian

Women', in Catherine Gallagher and Thomas Laqueur (eds.), *The Making of the Modern Body: Sexuality and Society in the Nineteenth Century*, Berkeley, CA: University of California Press.

Sánchez Albornoz, Nicolás, 1984, 'The Population of Colonial Spanish America', in Leslie Bethell (ed.), *The Cambridge History of Latin America*, Cambridge: Cambridge University Press.

Seed, Patricia, 1988, *To Love, Honor and Obey in Colonial Mexico*, Stanford, CA: Stanford University Press.

Silverblatt, Irene, 1987, *Moon, Sun and Witches: Gender Ideologies and Class in Inca and Colonial Peru*, Princeton, NJ: Princeton University Press.

Questioning Race and Gender in Post-Colonial Peru

FIONA WILSON

This study ocuses on the transition from colonialism to nationalism and seeks to explore how identities and relations of race and gender inherited from the colonial period were challenged and re-elaborated in the years following Independence when the Latin American nation state was established. By taking the case of Peru in the nineteenth century, the study will explore how the post colonial state approached issues of race and gender and will illustrate continuity and change from the history of one small Andean town where women and men as Indians, mestizos and whites, might stake out new identities, relations and collectivities but might also fight to shore up the old social order.

STATE DISCOURSES ON RACE AND GENDER IN NINETEENTH-CENTURY PERU

Colonial society throughout Latin America had been built on the notion that a socio-racial hierarchy existed through which social differences between colonised and coloniser were attributed to so-called racial and hence to allegedly inherent, natural and hereditary qualities (see Stolcke, this volume). The indigenous population (as well as others considered inferior by the Spanish) evaded, resisted and opposed white claims to power and the racist ideologies. Nevertheless, under the colonial social order, racism rested on a polarity between white and Indian/black women.[1] In the predominating narrative of the colonial era, women from white families were defined as chaste and virtuous and were subject to strict control by their families and by the religious orders they entered as nuns. Indian and black women, sexually abused by white men and forced into concubinage, were defined as promiscuous and without moral quality. Women had been made signifiers of morality and respectability by virtue of their race under the colonial social order.

Independence was won in Peru in 1824 by rebels of European descent fighting against the armies of Spain. The architects of the new Latin America wanted to do away with race as an organising principle of society. However, the liberators' dreams and the bodies of legislation passed did not mean that

Fiona Wilson, Centre for Development Research, Copenhagen, Denmark.

the socio–racial hierarchy, so long the foundation of the colonial order, could be swept away overnight. Officially, racial distinctions were a thing of the past. Use of the intricate codes to classify racial mixtures fell away; neither state nor church were to intervene or arbitrate on questions of racial purity in future. As a corollary, the indigenous population was no longer considered a separate juridical category and, according to the law, race was no longer to have a bearing on issues of property ownership or labour relations. In the euphoria of liberation, the state promised to end the demand for tribute from the Indian population but, by the same token, would no longer intervene as protectors of the indigenous communities threatened with encroachment by white settlers.

Liberation and emancipation were issues hotly debated by white intellectuals who, through the press and discussion circles in the capital, advocated social equality and lamented the abusive treatment that had been suffered by the humble Indian throughout the colonial period [*Wilson, 1990*]. To overcome the colonial heritage of backwardness and racial difference, education was taken to be the vital key. New social subjects could be created in schools run by secular authorities, open to girls as well as boys, and to Indians as well as mestizos and whites. But the nationalism emerging in nineteenth-century Latin America was to have complex and ambiguous implications for women and relations of gender. As Franco [*1989: 81*] has argued in the case of Mexico, national society needed to recode the position of women. Women were being recreated 'as mothers of the new men and as guardians of private life, which from Independence onward was increasingly seen as a shelter from political turmoil'. In Peru as in Mexico, this recodification led to a new emphasis on women's domestic identity and made purity and social respectability the responsibility of women.

However, ideas of nationalism, race and gender articulated by intellectuals in Lima (who had no direct contact with or understanding of Indian society) made slow headway. Only in the late nineteenth century were social relations being explored and analysed in more imaginative and radical ways in the Andean region, often by renegade sons of the white elite inspired by the political message of anarchism and Marxism then spreading in the continent [*Wilson, 1990*]. As far as most people living in the Andean region were concerned, control by a central state had faded away during most of the nineteenth century. 'Caudillos', with their bands of followers, competed for state power and it took several decades before the state was in a position to restore institutional control or before Lima could impose superior rule over the regional elites (indigenous as well as white). In the Andes, Independence had created an interlude – a hiatus – in the exercise of state power, and both indigenous society and the much reduced white elite in the provinces enjoyed new freedoms.

THE FIGHT OVER ANDEAN RESOURCES

The picture given in older works of Peruvian history is that the liberation struggles had left Peru poor, weak and conflict-ridden. True enough, the money
economy had been severely curtailed, many old Spanish property-owning families had left the provinces and haciendas turned inwards, producing only for
immediate use. However, the other history is that resources throughout the
Andean region were reappropriated by indigenous society and collapse of the
colonial regime had not heralded a retreat into subsistence or misery. On the
contrary, there was a resurgence of a vibrant indigenous economy (always present but suffering restriction and control by the colonial authorities) and a
renaissance of ethnic or regionally-based systems of production, deployment
of labour and circuits of exchange: see, for example, Samaniego [1978] and
Mallon [1983].

Corroborating this view of indigenous resurgence was the sharp increase in
the Indian population. Between 1790 and 1850 a larger proportion of
Peruvians (some 63 per cent) defined themselves as 'Indian' compared to any
time before or since [Gootenberg, 1991]. This suggests that boundaries
between indigenous and mestizo populations were far more fluid in practice
than racist interpretations would have one believe. Identification as Indian or
mestizo (an identity that stressed a mixed ancestry) was partly culture, partly
aspiration.

Liberal ideology was paramount and Peru's future was seen to lie in the
introduction of a market economy, expanded commodity production and free
trade. Resurgence of the indigenous economy and Indian identity did not go
unchallenged for long. White society received substantial reinforcements in
the shape of young men of European or American origin, who toured the
provinces in search of a fortune and who often sought to ally themselves
through marriage with property-owning families. White society started to put
up a stronger fight (backed up by armed force) to reappropriate the mines,
haciendas and other formerly Spanish–owned properties. Furthermore, expansion of white-directed commodity production from the mid-nineteenth century
led to renewed attacks on indigenous resources. The Indian population was
now faced with greater threats of dispossession than had been the case during
the Colony [Manrique, 1987; Jacobsen, 1993].

The struggle over resources waged in the Andes led to a keener interest on
the part of white society to preserve political control in the Andean regions, to
control communications (especially the new railways, telegraph and postal services linking Lima), and to coerce Indians into providing labour service. Given
Peru's typical boom/bust export economy, levels of financial disorder and frequent bankruptcy, impoverished central and provincial authorities once again
tried to claim the wealth produced by the indigenous economy, in spite of the

declared intention to end colonial tribute. Taxes on Indians were surreptitiously reintroduced under the new name of *contribuciones*.

In sum, one can suggest that, despite the ideas of liberation and emancipation accompanying the emergence of nationalism following Independence, the expansion of commodity production in the late nineteenth century tended to shore up ideologies of race and perpetuate relations of domination understood primarily in racist terms. However, there could be no going back to a colonial socio-racial order, for juridical and institutional structures underpinning racial distinctions had been removed. The management of race and gender relations was now in the hands of local society.

INTERSECTIONS OF RACE AND GENDER IN AN ANDEAN SOCIETY

The province of Tarma in the Central Andean region was a prosperous province located relatively close (some 230 kms) to Lima. An estimated 42,000 people lived in the province in 1876; about half that number clustering in the irrigated valleys surrounding the old colonial town of Tarma. The urban population was a mere 4,000 in 1876 but this figure probably did not include the Indian population living on the fringes of town. Urban society had long been the preserve of white property owners who controlled the municipal and political offices, that is, the Provincial Council and Prefecture. But the burgeoning regional economy in the late nineteenth century (with an increasing production of minerals and livestock from the highlands; aguardiente and coffee from the sub tropical zone as well as foodstuffs from the temperate heartland) not only led to a greater circulation of cash but also to the growing importance of Tarma town as an urban centre. The urban economy came to provide an ever increasing range of goods, services and opportunities and the town attracted many immigrants of local and foreign origins. This was to lead to the emergence of socio-economic classes and to generate new forms of political and social conflict (in which anarchist artisans and professionals fought against the land-owning elite).

Archival material is drawn upon to discuss three burning social issues in nineteenth century Tarma, which centred on the changing contours of race and gender. The first focuses on challenges to divisions of labour along gender and race lines found in the urban economy; the second reflects the penetration of new ideas about domesticity and consumption in the Andean provinces; and the third demonstrates changing attitudes and practices towards sexuality and inter-racial unions between whites and Indians.

(1) Challenging Divisions of Labour: Wholesalers and Shopkeepers

There is no doubt that in contemporary eyes the most visibly successful group of women earning a living in Tarma town were the wholesalers, described by one local newspaper as: 'those damned women who try our patience so much'. They acquired foodstuffs from the local peasantry and offered potatoes and maize, barley and beans, and many other goods besides, for sale on a daily basis. Both men and women sold meat and from the 1890s, coffee, tropical fruits and imported wheat flour brought from Lima were also found in the market-place. The presence of wholesalers in the Tarma market had been a recent phenomenon. No indigenous middlemen had been allowed to deal in the food market of the colonial towns, instead the peasantry had been obliged to come personally to town, attend church on Sundays and sell their goods in the urban market at prices fixed by custom and under the surveillance of the town's authorities.

By the late nineteenth century, the women's wholesaling businesses were being debated in the Provincial Council. Some members were inclined towards the arguments of trade liberalisation and put their trust in market forces to determine a fair price for the goods. They argued that the wholesalers worked for the benefit of the consuming public and committed no crime in the way they plied their trade. Others were not convinced; they claimed that the women made exorbitant profits by paying low prices to peasant producers yet charging high prices to the urban citizens. This faction wanted the town to go on controlling and policing the exchanges and warned that urban citizens were in danger of being held to ransom by the unscrupulous wholesalers.

While the debates raged about local free trade, wholesalers faced continued harassment from the town authorities who insisted on setting the prices of goods and raising municipal revenues through market dues. When in 1894 the Provincial Council voted to increase the levy, the women stopped trading in protest. Their action was labelled 'a strike' by the Lord Mayor. The women lodged complaints with both the Provincial Council and with the superior Departmental Junta in Cerro de Pasco. The Junta pronounced in favour of the women and demanded that the dues should be lowered and the proceeds devoted to improving market facilities.

Although the records never labelled them as 'Indians', the occupation of wholesaler in the Tarma market was strongly connected with an indigenous identity. First and foremost, the wholesalers bore the brunt of a lingering colonial attitude found amongst the white population, stressing that the peasantry had an obligation to supply cheap food to the town on account of their tributary status. This view was buttressed by the Provincial Council's claim throughout the nineteenth century that the town possessed inalienable rights over Indian land – that is, over communal lands of the indigenous communities which produced the staple food crop of potatoes but which, according to national law, were now under indigenous ownership.

Seen from this perspective, the wholesalers as Indians were supposed to provision the town without profit in return for the town authorities' protection of the communities. This proved a very convenient way of legitimising the differential treatment given to the trading groups operating in the town at the time. The Provincial Council's preoccupation with market women contrasts with a total lack of concern with respect to the male Italian and Chinese merchants in charge of the import trade who were never subject to scrutiny or control. Yet according to contemporary travellers, mark-ups of 200 to 300 per cent on imported luxury goods were common at the time. Foreign men were free to act in as profit-maximising a fashion as they could; indigenous women could not escape the long paternalistic arm of the authorities.

The market-place was where white and mestizo women were forced to confront Indian women directly on a daily basis and it appears that market relations became increasingly fraught and tense in the course of the century. In earlier periods, the white elite had not only owned haciendas, they had also developed links and networks with the local peasantry to exchange patronage and services for foodstuffs. However, the growth and diversification of the urban population had taken place at the same time as there was much greater competition for the foodstuffs produced around Tarma. Food shortages and price rises did occur with greater frequency and were blamed on the wholesalers. This tended to increase antagonisms and suspicions between women; women from the respectable white or mestizo families claimed they were cheated by the indigenous women wholesalers.

A second group of business women, whose activities expanded with the growth of the urban economy, were the shopkeepers. About a quarter of the 273 shops licensed in Tarma town between 1878 and 1906 were listed as belonging to women. Since only seven of these were widows, one may assume that the majority were shop-owners in their own right. Virtually all the women's shops belonged to the lowest category of commercial enterprise: that is, they were called *tiendas, pulperías* or *bodegas* – most were a mixture of small store and bar selling alcohol, coca and other basic goods to neighbours. By dealing in alcohol, the women shopkeepers also retained a strong identity with indigenous society. For generations, Indian women had been responsible for producing and distributing alcohol to the peasantry. This association continued even after cane-based alcohol was substituted for the home-made *chicha* and people had moved into town.

By contrast, respectable women from the white elite were never to be seen in the bars or billiard saloons thronging the town where their menfolk congregated and frequently drank to excess. Women found there were identified as prostitutes, and thus as promiscuous Indians. Dispensing alcohol could never be considered a decent or respectable trade for women.

In the case of both the wholesalers and the shopkeepers, one could argue that the presence of women in urban trading was related closely to the resurgence of the indigenous economy in that their activities formed part of wider family-based trading networks. We know that in the late nineteenth century indigenous traders were extremely active in trading foodstuffs from the temperate zones of Tarma to the mining centres located in high desolate spots above the limit of cultivation, as well as to the recently established plantations in the tropical zone to the east. From a base in town, Tarmeño muleteers spent much time carrying aguardiente from the tropical zone up to mines, haciendas, settlements and communities throughout the Sierra, where the demand for alcohol was growing rapidly. While men travelled the length and breadth of the province exchanging regional products, women were put in charge of the trading outlets in Tarma town.

Neither the wholesalers nor the women shopkeepers would have lived in the spatial domain of the white elite, that is, in the centre of town. Urban space was strongly and visibly segregated. They belonged to an urban periphery that had been relegated to indigenous/mestizo society. Apparently, this was where many of the women's enterprises were in fact located and where wholesalers gathered and stored their goods. Tarma's urban periphery had never been subject to the regulations which determined the grid-iron pattern of streets and urban services were not provided. Instead it was an agglomeration of thatch-roofed cottages, straggling up the steep hillsides, linked by narrow twisting paths. The population living in this indeterminate urban fringe had a shifting racial identity: they could define themselves or be defined as mestizos or indigenous in that they both held land and followed an urban trade. This was the kind of social group that might well have chosen an Indian identity earlier in the nineteenth century.

In the case of the strongest groups of women earning livelihoods in town, an overlapping of race with gender was used to separate them from 'true' urban society and, I wish to argue, these women continued to be imprisoned in the Indian and rural identities given them by white society to a far greater extent than men from a similar social background. They remained Indian partly on account of their work in a public place, and partly on account of the racial and gender associations of that work. Men appear to have had greater freedom to redefine their identities and to become accepted as mestizos. As traders, muleteers and artisans, men were more likely to find a place in urban society and be incorporated into the class structure emerging at the end of the nineteenth century.

(2) Changing Patterns of Domesticity and Consumption

Whether Indian, mestizo or white, women were the domestic managers of their households and took charge of child-rearing. They acquired, prepared and served food; acquired fuel and water and other household necessities; provided their families with clothing; and were responsible for furnishing and cleaning their houses. From the 1870s, the Provincial Council passed a mass of municipal ordinances in a self-conscious attempt to 'civilise' urban society and clean up the town. Numerous restrictions were placed on the households located in the white urban centre as to where and how they should dispose of rubbish, keep animals, do the household's washing, clean the street in front of the house.

Households were coerced into paying much greater attention to hygiene and cleanliness, partly in response to a growing fear of contagious diseases (such as typhus and plague). This served to expand the range of domestic labours and make them more time-consuming, especially for the white section of urban society. Barred from the Provincial Council, women had no say in the invasion of private space, nor could they influence the allocation of public money. Thus for many years, the building of a civic theatre was judged to be a more important objective by the men of the Provincial Council than the installation of a clean water supply.

The actual burden of women's domestic work diminished where there were servants, but the number of servants was no longer such a reliable indicator of social status as it had been in the past. By the mid-nineteenth century, conspicuous consumption had become the white population's most important yardstick demarcating their superiority to indigenous and mestizo society, and there were numerous opportunities for luxury consumption by mid-century.

During the 1870s, the staple foodstuff consumed by white families changed. Easier communication with the coast allowed the substitution of rice and imported wheat flour for the locally grown potatoes and maize. In the same period, Italian merchants profited greatly from the expanding demands of white society and brought to the Andes a vast array of extremely expensive goods imported from Europe. They offered clothes and shoes from London and Paris, Ceylon tea and Italian spaghetti, fine liquors and cigars, chocolates and sweets, perfumes and toothpaste, tins of tomato sauce and sardines, haberdashery and glassware, violins and writing materials.

If one compares consumption in the late nineteenth century with the colonial period, what seems to have changed is the way in which the new imports were aimed first and foremost at women. Men still prided themselves on their penchant for distinctive brands of expensive spirits and cigars. But for women, the new consumption culture seems to have become far more all-embracing. Elite women demonstrated their social superiority by the fashionable clothes worn, the luxury foods prepared, the European pastimes and the lavish furnishings of their houses. As a result, the gulf between white and indigenous/mestizo women grew. Even though the latter might possess considerable cash wealth, they did not adopt the trappings of a European life style, nor strive to distinguish their social position through consumption. Their aspirations were connected more with social mobility over the longer run. In this the education of their children was of paramount importance and they took advantage of the schools opening not only in Tarma town but in each of the districts and even on some of the haciendas.

(3) The Fate of Interracial Marriage

Family and property records in Tarma reflect how increasing numbers of white immigrants were coming to the Andes during the 1840s. It also appears that for a short period, perhaps only a mere 20 years, legitimate marriages were once again being contracted between European men and indigenous women. The reappearance of interracial marriage, for the first time since the very early years of the Spanish Colony, may have been linked to a general rejection of colonial racist ideologies. Furthermore, male migrants to the New World were coming from Europe and the Americas and had not themselves lived any experience of colonialism.

However, the cases of interracial marriage must also be seen in the light of the indigenous control of Andean resources at the time. Individual migrants, like the first generation of Spanish conquerors stood to benefit greatly by marrying into an upper land-holding strata of the indigenous peasantry as this was the way – usually the only way – of gaining access to land and labour. Given the bilateral inheritance system, indigenous women held property in their own right, but by the 1860s, a backlash was under way. Legal marriage between European men and indigenous women was made taboo; overt racism became rife.

We can take the case of one Tarmeño family of mixed descent by way of illustration. A young penniless Italian immigrant had arrived in the province in the 1840s and married a wealthy Indian woman who died soon after their only son was born. Taking over his dead wife's property, the Italian invested in a billiard saloon in the town. He then married a woman of German extraction whose family were coffee growers in the tropical zone and founded a second 'European' family. The son of the first marriage rose to become the leading merchant capitalist in the region who used kin and contacts to trade profitably between indigenous and white worlds. His European half-brothers, with whom relations were always strained, became hacendados.

The alleged racial impurity in this particular family was handled through resorting to the violent image of castration. Family anecdotes maintained that fathers castrated their sons, either because they were born (in wedlock) to indigenous mothers and had tainted blood (like the merchant capitalist son) or because sons of the European branch of the family wanted to defy family dictates and marry a woman considered racially inferior. It is hard to believe that castration was more than a terrible threat used to enforce obedience. Nevertheless, the men at the centre of the anecdotes had not (as far as was known) fathered children.

Restoration of a taboo against marriage between white men and Indian women may have had the effect of intensifying men's sexual interest in indigenous women. Young Indian women, who worked as household servants, were often sexually abused by the men in the house. And there seems also to have been a growing prevalence of concubinage. Men from the elite boasted about their illegitimate children and began more openly to support their second families economically. While respectable white wives were closeted in the domestic domain and were the chief bearers of the family's respectability, Indian and mestizo women were not only rivals for a husband's affections and money, they could be seen to possess greater freedom of movement and a greater measure of autonomy. Underlying jealousies exacerbated insecurities and tensions felt by white women in local society and they might become more openly and stridently racist than men.

A final note, however, is in order. In a provincial society like Tarma, one needs to be careful not to over-emphasise the white women's seclusion. As property owners, women, when widowed and sometimes also as wives of absent husbands, were frequently expected to act as the guardians of a family's patrimony and take charge of the management of haciendas and other properties [*Wilson, 1984*]. Many of these women were well-educated and highly independent; though notarial records also show that families placed legal restrictions on property-owning widows stopping them from marrying and in that way 'alienating' the dead husband's property.

BY WAY OF CONCLUSION

In this study I have tried to suggest that there had been an apparent softening of racial categories in early post-colonial Peru. Whether looked at from a national or regional perspective, the realities of indigenous economic and social prominence confounded white prejudice, privilege and wished-for dominance. Although colonial ideologies were under challenge and aspects of racial relations were being re-elaborated, nevertheless, the polarity between white and Indian women continued to be enforced, being re-fashioned in the course of the nineteenth century in line with the ideals and images connected with nationalism and changing economic and social situations.

This discussion has focused on the history of one small province in the Peruvian Andes. Yet the central points would seem to have wider applicability to Latin America and perhaps also be relevant to other post-colonial situations. Where racial classifications instigated and upheld by erstwhile colonial powers give way to a post-colonial social order then the practices of racism may be continued in ways that make even greater demands on women as bearers of racial and social status. Indeed, where no overt racist legislation exists greater use may be made of oppressive hierarchic gender relations which press women into acting as the principal, *de facto*, signifiers of racial or ethnic boundaries.

NOTES

1. In the text, the terms 'race', 'Indian' and 'white' are used to indicate meanings stemmning from the nineteenth century racial classification. For the sake of readability the inverted commas have been dropped.
2. The most important sources of archival data are the minutes of the debates of the Tarma Provincial Council; correspondence of the Lord Mayors of Tarma (complete from 1866); commercial licence records; tax schedules; notarial records on wills and property ownership; and local newspapers.

REFERENCES

Franco, Jean, 1989, *Plotting Women: Gender and Representation in Mexico*, London: Verso.
Gootenberg, Paul, 1991, 'Population and Ethnicity in early Republican Peru: Some Revisions', *Latin American Research Review*, Vol.26, No.3.
Jacobsen, Nils, 1993, *Mirages of Transition: The Peruvian Altiplano, 1780–1930*, Berkeley, CA: University of California Press.
Mallon, Florencia, 1983, *The Defense of Community in Peru's Central Highlands: Peasant Struggle and Capitalist Transition, 1860–1940*, Princeton, NJ: Princeton University Press.
Manrique, Nelson, 1987, *Mercado Interno y Región: La Sierra Central, 1820–1910*, Lima: DESCO.
Samaniego, Carlos, 1978, 'Peasant Movements at the Turn of the Century and the Rise of the Independent Farmer', in N. Long and B. Roberts (eds.), *Peasant Cooperation and Capitalist Expansion in Peru*, Austin, TX: University of Texas Press.
Wilson, Fiona, 1984, 'Marriage, Property, and the Position of Women in the Peruvian Central Andes', in R.T. Smith (ed.), *Kinship Ideology and Practice in Latin America*, Chapel Hill, NC: University of North Carolina Press.
Wilson, Fiona, 1990, 'Ethnicity and Race: Discussion of a Contested Domain in Latin American Thought', in S. Arnfred *et al.* (eds.), *The Language of Development*, Copenhagen: New Social Science Monographs.

The Ethnicisation of Politics and the Politicisation of Ethnicity: Culture and Political Development in South Africa

PREBEN KAARSHOLM

In my opinion, gender and ethnicity do not sit easily together on an agenda for discussion. They seem to constitute different layers or levels within the complex of multiple identities and bases for cultural and political mobilisation that we are really discussing. In a context of overlapping, fluctuating, shifting and mutually interlinked identifications that are made in accordance with signifiers like class, language, religion, caste, generation, clan affiliation, social movement or ideological attachment, or whatever other register might be set as relevant, gender appears to constitute a more basic level of identity of differentiation, that underlies and interacts with other layers but presents different problems for discussions of politicisation. Thus, in his book *The Remembered Village*, the Indian anthropologist, M.N. Srinivas, describes how differences of gender could overrule those of caste and religion in his Mysore village, even as the chaos of partition was culminating in 1947–48 [*Srinivas, 1976: 249*]. Norma Kriger, in her recent study of struggles during the Zimbabwean decolonisation war, demonstrates that of all the fronts opened up in the war between generations, lineages, and so on, the gender front was the one where change was least [*Kriger, 1991: 137–9*].[1] Thus, while it makes sense to discuss how gender gets modelled and articulated through discourses of ethnicity, it is misleading to think of gender and ethnicity as constituting parallel types of 'primordial identity' which can be theorised and approached methodologically in the same way.

In this article, I shall focus primarily on ethnicity as a level of discourse, identification and creation of difference drawn upon and prioritised in processes of political mobilisation, and I shall consider some of the consequences such politicisation may have for the understanding and function of ethnicity.

According to the assumptions of 'classical' modernisation theory stemming from American and West European thinking about relations between economic, social, political and cultural development of the 1950s and 1960s, 'traditional' cultural differentiations and the ascription of particular social functions to particular social groups would become eroded in the process of

Preben Kaarsholm, International Development Studies, Roskilde University Centre, Denmark.

economic modernisation. These would give way to anonymous, individualised and empathy-oriented modes of outlook and self-understanding which would provide the precondition for the emergence of modern types of participatory and equality-based systems of political representation and government [*Apter, 1965; Lerner, 1968; Morse, 1969*]. This was seen as a unidirectional process which was in some ways 'tragic' inasmuch as it replaced a world of dense cultural riches with an 'iron cage' of secularised rationality and atomisation. More importantly, it was seen as capable of liberating human potential from the shackles of arbitrarily assigned ascriptions and limitations [*Weber, 1985*]. A similarly unidirectional view has been characteristic of Marxist theories of modernisation, which have tended to regard ethnicity, not so much as a 'genie in a bottle' [*Marks, 1992*], but rather as a backward-looking, semi-fascist devil belonging to a world of ideology and rural idiocy which the development of productive forces would replace by one of rational class struggle and universalised notions of what constitutes oppression and freedom. Thus already in 1848, Frederick Engels could ridicule Scandinavianism as a particularly retrograde mode of thinking, as drunken barbarism and brutality against women masked by sentimentality soaked in tears.[2]

The paradigmatic and unidirectional character of both these models has been undermined, however, by the extremely varied and broken ways in which modernisation has progressed in different parts of the world. Any direct relation between base and superstructure, or between economic accumulation and increasing equality, participation or socialist revolutionary potential now appears to be the exception rather than the rule. On the one hand, people in a variety of cases have sought refuge in modes of cultural identification and differentiation in order to defend themselves against the uneven consequences of modernity rather than enjoy its unsettling and liberating effects. On the other hand, political regimes have been able to use with considerable success strategies of cultural separation to consolidate power and control.

This process of reacting or adjusting to modernisation in ways which are diametrically opposed to the assumptions of modernisation theory in its two major 'classical' variants has manifested itself in societies where programmes of economic development have failed as well as in societies where development has generated accumulation, but has been accompanied by strong differentiation in income and social welfare.

It would be interesting to make a comparative study of the mobilisation potential of ethnicity and cultural differentiation. One could look at state control and popular resistance in some countries where hopes of modernisation have been spectacularly frustrated, like Uganda or Bangladesh, and in other countries where modernisation has been successful, but also highly uneven and divisive, like Brazil, Malaysia or South Africa, where traditional networks for securing reproduction have broken down.

South Africa is a particularly interesting case, since here ethnicity was deployed much more openly and programmatically within a colonial project of partial modernisation, as a strategy for state control and social engineering, than anywhere else in the world, including Israel and Malaysia. At the same time, in South Africa, ethnicity has crystallised out as an issue in opposition to other forms of politics in a particularly clear-cut way which seems to confront two diametrically opposed conceptions of how popular aspirations are articulated most authentically and representatively. The views are so radically opposed that the battle between them threatens to destroy the basis for developing *any* kind of democratic political culture in South Africa, which for this very reason is being fomented and manipulated by forces whose manifest interest rests with an absence of democracy.

One principal position is represented by the 'classical' unifying nationalism of the ANC, striving for an equal-vote-based, non-racial, democratic constitution and the building of an undivided nation. For the opposing position, its most radical and coherent argument has been formulated by the Conservative Party and its chairman Andries Treurnicht. In an attempt to win international sympathy, the break-up of the Soviet Union into federalism and subnationalist politics was linked with South Africa. Shortly before his death, Treurnicht told readers of the *International Herald Tribune* that:

> The ethnic awakening and demand for self-determination in Eastern Europe has been political practice in South Africa for the past four decades, but is now being betrayed [by a democratic dispensation where numbers necessarily will decide] ... South Africa has a deeply divided population – along racial, ethnic, cultural, language and religious lines ... To force together such largely disparate people, cultures and races, will amount to a form of tyranny, the very opposite of democratic freedom ... [instead we must promote] the development of separate freedoms for the various peoples, ethnic groups, in their own territories, or homelands.[3]

In this way, conservative adherents of apartheid can pose as representatives of 'the new': of a post-modern, cultural relativistic view of politics as opposed to the old-fashioned centralised, modernist and tyrannically rationalist and Jacobin nationalist ANC.

While this contradiction between the centralised nationalism of the ANC and the ethnic nationalism of the Conservative Party is straightforward, the position of the Inkatha Freedom Party (IFP), trying to establish itself as representing a position alternative to both, is much more ambiguous. In the process of redefining itself from a 'cultural movement' to a 'freedom party', Inkatha has toned down, in its public statements, the ethnic components in its programme and emphasised instead the organisation's ambition to further free enterprise and political liberalism along lines which should water the mouth of any potential foreign investor if such still exist. The preservation of cultural values continues to figure prominently on the agenda, but in a pluralist formulation: 'to promote and support worthy customs and cultures of all South Africans'. And the party is obviously keen to remodel its public image from one of Zulu cultural nationalism to one of a more all-embracing national representativeness. Thus at the Annual General Meeting of the IFP, which I had the opportunity to attend at Ulundi in July 1991, all speeches were given in three languages – Zulu, Sotho and English – and there were violent protests from delegates when Tom Langley of the Conservative Party tried to address the meeting as one of 'the Zulu nation' and convey greetings from 'the Afrikaner nation'. 'We are not Zulus!', came the horrified shouts of white Inkatha members.

In other aspects of its political discourse, its symbolism and style of rhetoric and its everyday practice of mobilisation, however, there can be no doubt about Inkatha's ethnic strategies. While the meeting at Ulundi was being treated to visions of peaceful pluralist democracy, *impi* warriors armed with 'cultural weapons' and uniformed Youth and Women's Brigades were dancing defiantly outside the big tents. Each time the President rose to speak he was preceded by praise poets who would at great length extol his merits as the figurehead of black African political aspirations.

More than anything, Inkatha has worked to counteract support for the ANC in local constituencies. This has been done to a large extent by urging and pressing people to organise along ethnic lines in opposition to the 'communism' and universalism of the ANC. With the support of the South African Police and the South African Defence Force, Inkatha has thus managed to divide the townships of the Rand and the tracts of Natal into opposing camps violently fighting each other. They subscribe not only to different political programmes, but to radically different ideas of what constitutes political culture and the basic premises for political interaction. Most tragically, perhaps, Inkatha has forced sections of the ANC into thinking and reacting according to the same patterns of violent camp politics and to take on the premises of its adversary [*Trewhela, 1991*].

In this way, the battle between a monadic apartheid conception of politics and a universalist democratic one has been moved into the heartlands of black African communities and, as Shula Marks [*1992*] has pointed out, the battle has been intensified by the 'power vacuum' created by increased destabilisation and economic crisis, the gradual dismantling of formal and legal apartheid measures of social control and, paradoxically, by the growing possibilities for a transition from minority to majority rule.

The situation, however, is not just one of a 'power vacuum', but also of an 'ideology vacuum', or, to put it differently, of a crisis of political discourse.

The Indian political scientist Sudipta Kaviraj has recently described how centralised nationalist discourse in India has disintegrated from an earlier situation around independence when nationalist leaders were able to mediate between national and regional languages of politics and the dialects of local community political aspirations. In later years, nationalist discourse has ballooned away from the understandings and articulations of ordinary people and has become the exclusive domain of elite politicians. In this way, a rupture has opened between an increasingly abstract sense of national belonging and other forms of communalist identity. Where previously ethnicity, like other layers of multiple identity, had a 'fuzzy' nature which allowed it to be interwoven flexibly with other strands of identity formation and mobilisation, it now aspires to being a *monopolising* force that excludes and supersedes other markers of identity [*Kaviraj, 1992a; Kaviraj, 1992b; Chatterjee, 1992*].

South Africa is obviously different from India. But there might still be parallels in the way relations between nationalism and ethnicity have developed over the last decades if one compares the generation of nationalist leaders like Nehru and Luthuli with the present generation of leaders returning to local politics from the outside, from exile or from prison.[6] In any case, it seems risky to view the battle between the political discourses of nationalism on the one hand, and crystallised ethnicity on the other, solely as the outcome of state intervention and manipulation. There can be no doubt that the discourse of centralised African nationalism with a socialist orientation that came to the fore in the 1980s has in many ways become problematic, due to its banishment from the internal South African scene, the development of corrupt absolutism along nationalist lines in other African countries, and the collapse of the 'socialist' societies of Eastern Europe and the Soviet Union. At present the contours of an alternative discourse of democratic nationalism or regionalism are still very vague.

Neither is there any doubt that when a transition to majority rule comes about and an ANC-led government achieves power, such a government will face overwhelming problems of restructuring, redistribution and securing investment in a context of economic crisis, intensified urbanisation and pressure on resources resulting from the dismantling of apartheid. It is difficult to be optimistic in a situation where the institutions of political culture have been so systematically eroded, and violence has ruled for so long.

So although policies of ethnic differentiation have been discredited as parts of apartheid strategy, and Inkatha compromised by its close links with the pre-apartheid state authorities, it is hard to imagine how hardened ethnicities will not play a prominent part in the political mobilisation of South African politics in future. This obviously cannot be prevented by repressing or outlawing ethnic political organisation. Hopefully it may take place in circumstances where the basic premises of political culture are not broken up along lines of communalist separation, but rather within an institutional framework in which ethnic political parties and organisations compete for influence with parties and organisations basing themselves on different programmes and discourses.

In this way the most fundamental struggle in South Africa appears to be one over the basic values and institutions of political culture. Only where there is a minimum of tolerance and some structures for the mediation of conflict through communication and acceptance of basic procedural rules for negotiation can one hope for a 'resoftening' of ethnicity. A demobilisation of its violent and xenophobic forms is needed and a new distancing and relativisation of notions of ethnicity that will allow them to interact constructively with other backgrounds to mobilisation.

It should not be forgotten that such modern notions of ironically distanced ethnicity are already strongly present in the popular culture of South Africa, where ethnic culture has been reduced to and compartmentalised as folklore, or where an ethnic idiom is played upon to give special resonance to humour, irony or affection in otherwise 'uprooted' and culturally mixed genres of expression. Examples of this are the ways in which elements of Zulu culture have been reworked by *mbube* choirs[7] or by an *mbaqanga* group like Mahlathini and the Mahotella Queens to express messages which are both familiar and comprehensible and critically new. The image of the leopard skin-clad Mahlathini only being able to stay on his feet spiritually and physically, due to the support of his three powerful Mahotella Queens, presents a redeeming antidote to ideological notions of Zulu patriarchy which revitalise and change the status of the idiom rather than dismiss it.[8]

In contrast with an earlier period where it was possible to understand oneself both as a Zulu proud of one's cultural background and resistance history and as an ANC nationalist mobilising for a South Africa liberated from apartheid, the late 1970s and the 1980s brought about a confrontation between centralised and ethnic nationalism. The combination of an Inkatha offensive challenging the hegemony of organisations supporting the ANC in African politics and the banishment of the major African nationalist movements from the internal political scene led to the emergence of irreconcilably differentiated types of self-understanding. Already during the Soweto uprising of 1976, there were violent clashes between township youth supporting the rebellion and the inhabitants of ethnically segregated hostels who wanted to stay out of the fray. As such confrontations became more widespread, fuelled by the interventions of state agents, the ANC became increasingly 'modern' and anti-ethnic in its outlook and formulations. The roots for ethnic mobilisation were dismissed as simply reactionary or as the outcome of manipulations by a conspiracy of white apartheid and opportunist *bantustan* politicians. A good example of this type of analysis is provided by Mzala's book on Chief Buthelezi from 1988 which does not recognise any kind of unforced popular support for the ethnic nationalism represented by Inkatha [*Mzala, 1988*].

Such an analysis was one-sided and reductionist, and it overlooked the extent to which the ANC and the centralist nationalism it represented had become an abstraction in the everyday life and politics of black South Africans. In exile, and with its great unifying leader imprisoned, the political thinking of the ANC tended to petrify around notions, arguments and ideas of leadership. It was not being challenged and rethought within left opposition movements as elsewhere in the world. Thus, instead of understanding the challenge of ethnic nationalist mobilisation dialectically as the outcome of both conservative manipulation and grassroots frustration, the ANC tended to dismiss the ethnicisation of politics out of hand. The ANC countered it with a programme of democratic nation-building for the whole of South Africa, which did not take community differentiation and grievances of communication into account and provided little more than abstract meaning and a set of symbolic rallying points for local constituencies. At the same time, the post-1985 campaign to make local communities 'ungovernable' and set up alternative structures of counter-hegemony on behalf of the ANC 'camp', parallel with the separatist offensive of Inkatha, served to confront centralist and ethnic nationalism as irreconcilably different platforms for mobilisation and to escalate the violence, undermining possibilities for the development of a democratic political culture.

Only belatedly did the ANC begin to take the ethnic challenge seriously. It has been attempting through the Congress of Traditional Leaders of South Africa (CONTRALESA) and new tactical alliances with some of the homelands' governments to challenge Inkatha's usurpation and monopolisation of 'traditional' and ethnic articulations and potentials. This coincided, more or less, with the first attempts within the ANC to come to terms with the upheavals and clamours for democratic reform which in the late 1980s were erupting with unpredictable force in Eastern Europe and the Soviet Union. These forced the organisation to confront critically the ideological legacy of 'the Second World' that had provided its main moral, political and economic support throughout the period of exile, and thereby also the 'centralism' of its own leadership within the struggle for a democratic South Africa.

Thus, in a 1989 working paper, Joe Slovo, the general secretary of the South African Communist Party and former head of Umkonto we Ziswe (the ANC's military wing), critically addressed the dogmatism which had come to characterise the political theory of the South African left and its reliance on outdated and disputable notions of the need for a 'dictatorship of the proletariat', a 'vanguard party' and the benefit of a one-party state to replace the apartheid caricature of 'bourgeois' parliamentary democracy [*Slovo, 1989*]. Slovo criticised further policies based on the 'big bang theory of socialism' and argued that 'many ingredients of social systems which succeed one another ... cannot be separated by a Chinese Wall'. The outcome of his argument was that the nationalist and socialist struggle must be one for 'multi-party post-apartheid democracy' and for 'political pluralism' involving a guarantee for all citizens of 'the basic rights and freedoms of organisation, speech, thought, press, movement, residence, conscience, and religion'.

Slovo's paper, however, said little about how these values and goals could be promoted at the present time and it is not clear from his formulations to what extent ethnic forms of organisation and mobilisation would be acceptable elements of the new pluralism. Concerning such issues, 'Preparing for Freedom', an ANC discussion paper prepared by Albie Sachs in late 1989, is more articulate and provocative. For Sachs [1990: 24], 'the method is the message' in the struggle against apartheid. This implies that pluralism must be not only a distant goal for the future, but also a characteristic of nationalist political mobilisation here and now:

> ... we exercise true leadership in being non-hegemonic, by selflessly trying to create the widest unity of the oppressed and to encourage all forces for change, by showing the people that we are fighting not to impose a view upon them but to give them the right to choose the kind of society they want and the kind of government they want [ibid.: 28].

The call is not:

> for a homogenised South Africa made up of identikit citizens ... we [must] envisage [South Africa] as a multi-lingual country. It will be multi-faith and multi-cultural as well. The objective is not to create a model culture into which everyone has to assimilate, but to acknowledge and take pride in the cultural variety of our people. In the past, attempts were made to force everyone into the mould of the English gentleman, projected as the epitome of civilisation, so that it was an honour to be oppressed by the English. Apartheid philosophy, on the other hand, denied any common humanity and insisted that people be compartmentalised into groups forcibly kept apart. In rejecting apartheid, we do not envisage a return to a modified form of the British imperialist notion, we de not plan to build a non-racial yuppiedom which people may enter only by shedding and suppressing the cultural heritage of their specific community [ibid.: 24ff].

On the other hand, Sachs refuses to accept, either in the struggle or in the envisaged future democratic dispensation, forms of 'tribal chauvinism' and 'ethnic exclusiveness' [ibid.: 26–7] which do not recognise a minimum set of nationally universal institutions, rights and regulations within 'a single South Africa' [ibid.: 24].

While the unified nation is still the fundamental frame of reference for political imagination, and the boundaries between 'exclusive' and legitimate ethnic organisation may be difficult to draw exactly, Albie Sachs' paper does appear to draw up an agenda for a new and different political culture. In the context of this vision, one could imagine an 'unhardening' of ethnicity that would allow it to act as a focus for organisation and even as the basis for the founding of certain political parties existing alongside organisations, bringing people together according to alternative criteria of social identity.

Another tendency that might help, paradoxically, to further an 'unhardening' of ethnicity, is the growing awareness of how some ethnic organisations have been turned into direct instruments of state violence against the opposition in South Africa. The hearings of the Goldstone Commission and the stubborn journalistic campaigns carried in the *Weekly Mail*, the *New Nation* and the *Vrye Weekblad* have unearthed increasing evidence that the South African Police and the South African Defence Force have been co-operating extensively with the Inkatha Freedom Party in an effort to ethnicise the premises of township politics and provoke confrontations between Zulus and Xhosas. Typically this has taken the form of mobilising or pressuring hostel-dwelling migrant labourers into joining hit squads, trained by police or army personnel to attack ANC meetings, leaders or sympathisers, and to engage in random violence and killing with the intention of destabilising any 'normal' peaceful build-up of oppositional political culture and procedure in black African communities.[9]

The immediate outcome of such bloody intervention and ethnicisation of politics is to make the establishment of a tolerant and pluralist alternative political culture along Albie Sachsian lines extremely difficult. The more long-term effect, if the violence is brought under control and its background fully clarified, might be to expose the joint Inkatha–South African security force mobilisation as representing a very particular type of politicisation of ethnicity that is highly destructive of other forms of locality – and language-based loyalties. The exposure and awareness of the special character of Inkatha's use of ethnicity for state manipulation might in the end help open up the political field to other varieties of ethnic discourse and organisation of a more peaceful and 'unhardened' type that would be able to interact with other groups within the framework of a commonly agreed political cultural consensus.

The importance of taking ethnicity and locally-based cultures and political languages seriously is related to the need to enter a dialogue with, and represent, some of the poorest, weakest groups in society. The rural proletariat, migrant workers and, not least, women have only had restricted access to education and to central national languages. Their needs often remain unarticulated and disregarded unless local languages and cultural terms of reference are taken into account. This is a point that has recently been made by Luke Mhlaba, convincingly, in the context of political and cultural development in

Zimbabwe [*Mhlaba, 1991: 209–25*]. Mhlaba argues for the importance of supporting the development of local language strategies in education, media production and cultural policy in order to provide democratic possibilities for all groups in society. He also sees the necessity of reducing the concentration of political power at central state level and of working towards more federalist forms of government with a high degree of power delegated to provincial and local levels.

Federalism in the case of South Africa has earned a bad name because of its association with the racist and economically unjust union of semi-independent 'homelands', and because of the belief in the necessity for 'a single South Africa', a firm credo of African nationalist and anti-apartheid politicians. However, future developments in the greater Southern African region might bring into question, in a new way, the representational and economic adequacy of present political boundaries and national state levels. If South Africa is democratised and restrictions on trade, investment and other forms of economic interaction are reduced, it might make sense to reduce the influence of present-day nation-states in favour of new institutions of government built up at the regional level. This, in turn, would require that a substantial reform and expansion of representational and administrative institutions take place at the local level, which might provide the opportunity for rethinking the issue of federalism with a view to providing political structures with a higher degree of legitimacy and responsiveness *vis-à-vis* the poorest and weakest groups in society. Such a development might help to dismantle and 'unharden' the opposition between nationalist and ethnic political principles as it exists today and would demand that nationalist politicians develop both programmes and discourses that are more sensitive to local needs and understandings.

The speeches and documents presented at the Ulundi Annual General Meeting of the Inkatha Freedom Party in 1991 demonstrated an awareness on the part of Chief Buthelezi and his organisation that groups such as women, who are weak in terms of access to national cultural resources, provide them with a particularly promising base for recruitment. Thus, in the section of his main speech dealing with 'The Role of Women in the Politics of Change', Buthelezi emphasised the special relationship which exists between himself as leader and the women of his party: 'In the IFP women have always been the backbone of my political support, and of the resilience of our Party... If women allow themselves to be dragged on behind male-dominated political Parties, they will be authoring their own deprivation in the future.'[10] At the same time, in spite of these almost feminist exhortations, the messages addressed to women also demonstrated how central gender issues are in the construction of ethnic political ideology. Thus, when Buthelezi referred to 'a whole new social class of persons' having been brought into being by apartheid, 'the unmarried black mothers', he was activating the ideological tenets of the family and the homestead and upholding the virtues of a cultural traditionalism which have come under threat from both a 'modernist' government and from left nationalist politicians who are betraying their cultural roots.[11]

While gender and ethnicity do thus represent types of identity formation that are different in many ways and require different exploratory approaches, they also represent ideological registers and discourses that may be interwoven in the terrain of local everyday-life politics. If this terrain is neglected as an arena for articulation and interaction by nationalist politicians, it is left open for co-optation and monopolisation by other forces whose aims in ethnicising politics are not those of working towards democracy.

NOTES

1. A rich material of insight into women's experiences of war and national liberation in Zimbabwe is offered by the 30 interviews in Staunton [*1990*]. On gender and cultural tradition in Rhodesia and Zimbabwe, see the remarkable novel by Dangarembga [*1988*].
2. Der Skandinavismus besteht in der Begeisterung für die brutale, schmutzige, seeräuberische, altnordische Nationalität, für jene tiefe Innerlichkeit, die ihre überschwenglichen Gedanken und Gefühle nicht in Worte bringen kann, wohl aber in Taten, nämlich in Roheit gegen Frauenzimmer, permanente Betrunkenheit und mit tränenreicher Sentimentalität abwechselnde Berserkerwut [*Engels, 1975: 394*].
3. *International Herald Tribune* (Singapore edition), 2 March 1990.
4. See, for example, 'Negotiations for Life and Democracy or Conflict and Destruction – Message by the President: Mangosuthu G. Buthelezi', Inkatha Freedom Party Annual General Conference, Ulundi, Saturday, 20 July 1991.
5. Inkatha Freedom Party Constitution, undated, Ch.1, 1.12, p.2.
6. On Luthuli as African nationalist and Zulu leader, see Marks [*1992*].
7. See Erlmann [*1991*]. For *mbube* singing in Zimbabwe, see Kaarsholm [*1990: 256*].
8. Listen, for example, to the song 'Stop Crying – Be a Man!' on the record Mbaqanga by Mahlathini and the Mahotella Queens (*Gallo BL742, 1991*).
9. The *Weekly Mail, New Nation* and *Vrye Weekblad* campaigns revealing co–operation between Inkatha and the South African Police and Security Forces were launched on 19 July 1991, on the eve of the Annual General Meeting of the Inkatha Freedom Party at Ulundi. Since then almost every new issue of the journals has contained fresh testimonies and evidence of such a conspiracy of violent destabilisation and its inspiration by similar murderous practices during the last years of Rhodesia and in Namibia and Mozambique in the 1980s. On this latter aspect, see, for example, Koch [*1992: 6–7*]. On Inkatha involvement in attacks on Soweto commuter trains, see Rulashe [*1992: 5*].
10. Mangosuthu G. Buthelezi, 'Negotiations for Life and Democracy or Conflict and Destruction. Message by the President ...', *op. cit.*, p.13. The special and direct relationship between 'the Leader' and members of the Inkatha 'Women's Brigade' is underlined similarly in the Inkatha Freedom Party *Constitution*, op. cit., p.7.
11. *Ibid.*, p. 12.

REFERENCES

Apter, D. E., 1965, *The Politics of Modernization*, Chicago, IL: University of Chicago Press.
Chatterjee, Partha, 1992, 'The Agenda for Nationalism', in P. Kaarsholm (ed.), *Popular Movements,*

Political Organisation, Democracy and the State, Occasional Paper No.4, Roskilde: International Development Studies.

Dangarembga, Tsitsi, 1988, *Nervous Conditions*, London: The Women's Press.

Engels, Friedrich, 1975, 'Der dänisch-preussische Waffenstillstand', *Neue Rheinische Zeitung*, 10 Sept. 1848, in Karl Marx and Friedrich Engels, *Werke, Vol.5*, Berlin: Dietz Verlag.

Erlmann, Veit, 1991, *African Stars: Studies in Black South African Performance*, Chicago: University of Chicago Press.

Kaarsholm, Preben, 1990, 'Mental Colonisation or Catharsis? Theatre, Democracy and Cultural Struggle from Rhodesia to Zimbabwe', *Journal of Southern African Studies*, Vol.16, No.2.

Kaarsholm, Preben (ed.), 1991, *Cultural Struggle & Development in Southern Africa*, London and Harare: James Currey and Baobab Books.

Kaviraj, Sudipta, 1992a, 'On State, Society and Discourse in India', in James Manor (ed.), *Rethinking Third World Politics*, London: Longman.

Kaviraj, Sudipta, 1992b, 'The Imaginary Institution of India', in P. Chatterjee and G. Pandey (eds.), *Subaltern Studies*, Vol.VII.

Koch, Eddie, 1992, 'Dance Macabre of Colonels and Inyangas', *Weekly Mail*, Vol.8, No.16, pp.6–7.

Kriger, N., 1991, 'Popular Struggles in Zimbabwe's War of National Liberation', in Kaarsholm (ed.) [*1991*].

Lerner, D., 1968, 'Modernization: Social Aspects', in D.L. Sills (ed.), *International Encyclopedia of the Social Sciences*, Vol.9, New York: Macmillan.

Marks, Shula, 1992, 'The Origins of Ethnic Violence in South Africa', in P. Kaarsholm (ed.), *Institutions, Culture and Change at Local Community Level*, Occasional Paper No.3, Roskilde: International Development Studies.

Mhlaba, Luke, 1991, 'Local Cultures and Development in Zimbabwe: The Case of Matabeleland', in P. Kaarsholm (ed.) [*1991*].

Morse, C. *et al.*, 1969, *Modernization by Design: Social Change in the Twentieth Century*, Ithaca, NY: Cornell University Press.

Mzala, 1988, *Buthelezi: Chief with a Double Agenda*, London: Zed Press.

Rulashe, Linda, 1992, 'Witness 01 Tells of Inkatha Hit–Men', *Weekly Mail*, Vol.8, No.21, p.5.

Sachs, Albie, 1990, 'Preparing for Freedom', *Weekly Mail*, reprinted in Ingrid de Kok and Karen Press (eds.), *Spring is Rebellious: Arguments about Cultural Freedom by Albie Sachs and Respondents*, Cape Town: Buchu Books.

Slovo, Joe, 1989, 'Has Socialism Failed?', mimeograph, Johannesburg: ANC.

Srinivas, M. L., 1976, *The Remembered Village*, Delhi: Oxford University Press.

Staunton, Irene (ed.), 1990, *Mothers of the Revolution*, Harare: Baobab Books.

Trewhela, Paul, 1991, 'The Trial of Winnie Mandela', *Searchlight South Africa*, Vol.2, No.3.

Weber, Max, 1985, *The Protestant Ethic and the Spirit of Capitalism*, London: Allen & Unwin.

Ethnicity and Gender in Zambia: What Kind of a Relationship?

KAREN TRANBERG HANSEN

This contribution explores the relationship between ethnicity and gender in Zambia, the former British colony of Northern Rhodesia. I first give a very summarised version of how some anthropologists have sought to come to terms with ethnicity during the colonial period, then I suggest why their view is limited and, following my own suggestions, I seek to tease out the place of ethnicity in post-colonial society. I will also try to find a place for gender in the process, if I can.

ETHNICITY IN NORTHERN RHODESIA

The colonial administration in Northern Rhodesia drew many of its policies from South Africa. The colony's largely mineral-based economy was under-pinned by an enforced rural/urban gender division of labour in which African men performed urban wage labour and African women maintained fields and rural households. Unlike in South Africa, the African urban population came from a large number of relatively small groups, resulting in a very varied urban population mix. These groups were not obviously different in culture. The major markers between them were rather in the social-organisational realm, such as distinctions between matrilineal and patrilineal groups. As in South Africa, urban housing for Africans was almost entirely under the control of employers (for example, mines; railways) or local authorities. Such housing was allotted by administrative fiat, that is, when vacancies occurred, and it was based neither on regional background nor on personal choice. You took what you got. In short, in Northern Rhodesia there were none of the 'tribal' com-pounds or urban ethnic concentrations that we have learned about from South Africa. Although African women were not supposed to be in towns, they kept leaving the villages. There was also a good deal of inter-ethnic marriage. The mining companies made 'married housing' available in Broken Hill (now Kabwe) in the 1930s and in the Copperbelt in the 1940s, assuming that a worker was likely to be more steady, if not more productive, when he had domestic services provided by a wife rather than by a prostitute [*Heisler, 1974*].

Karen Tranberg Hansen, Department of Anthropology, Northwestern University, Evanston, Illinois, USA.

Anthropologists who conducted research in the mining towns showed that questions pertaining to workers' economic livelihoods, rather than their particularistic affiliations, overrode 'tribal', or home region connections. This does not mean that such connections were absent, but that African urban politics were labour-oriented [Epstein, 1958].

Most scholarship conducted on these towns during the colonial period has viewed ethnicity as a matter of inter-group relations rather than as personal identity, which is to say as categorical indicators involving both ethnic and regional characteristics with overlapping meanings [Mitchell, 1956]. This kind of ethnicity sorted the urban mix into people farther from, or closer to home, both in physical distance and social terms: those with whom one could joke, and those whom one could not marry. As a means of steering a worker's way through the urban heterogeneity, this categorical ethnicity was also situational, determined principally, as Gluckman and Mitchell [1966] argued, by the new requirements which urban working life imposed on Africans. Once in the village, our worker turned tribesman.

Many contemporaries considered Gluckman's [1961] oft-quoted statement, 'an African miner is a miner; an African tribesman is a tribesman', to be radical because it suggested a 'modern' way of explaining urban African behaviour, with urban tribalism (Gluckman's terms) operating as a kind of sorting device that bore little resemblance to rural tribalism. Yet more recent scholarship has argued that this view is part of a 'grand modernist narrative' that hides essential dimensions of African interaction (including ethnicity) from view [Ferguson, 1990–91]. While I agree that much work needs to be done to theorise the dynamic place of African 'traditions' in their confrontation with new powers, the task of unravelling the effects of colonial power (and their postcolonial successors) on subject peoples remains equally challenging. Regarding the latter, I suggest that the power differential between the European colonisers and their African subjects, especially in the legal and technological realms, warrants more attention because these realms helped to shape the terms on which Africans reconstituted inter-group relationships.

The colonial administration and anthropologists also took note of an ethnic division of labour regarding wage labour, in that some groups tended to be better represented in certain lines of work than others. For example, 'Nyassas', that is, men from Nyasaland and the eastern parts of Northern Rhodesia, were more likely to work as clerks than were men from the extreme north-western part of the colony, like the Balovale, among whom many worked as night-soil removers. The African messenger corps had a considerable element of Ngoni men who were held to have a 'warrior tradition', and the Bemba were considered too 'warlike' to undertake the tedious work of domestic service [Epstein, 1975; Matejko, 1976]. And so on.

Wage labour during the colonial period was first and foremost men's work, yet women from some distinct ethnic groups clustered in particular occupations. Almost every town had its special prostitutes, whose common characteristic was that they were from a 'different' locality. On the Copperbelt, you had 'Kasai' women from Congo, as well as Lamba women from the rural reserve [*Siegel, 1989*]. Ila women were reported to frequent Broken Hill and Lusaka [*Evans, 1950*]. The Great East Road that made Lusaka into a port town for eastern province migrants was known as a busy conveyor belt for prostitutes. And Lozi chiefs made many trips to Livingstone to round up women [*Hansen, 1989: 110–20*].

Studies of ethnic distance and occupational ranking by urban Africans carried out under the auspices of the Rhodes-Livingstone Institute revealed a connection between the ranking of jobs and of ethnic groups [*Mitchell, 1956; 1987: 180–242*]. The common sense perceptions, held both by some Europeans and some Africans, about the characteristics of others, do indeed constitute ethnicity of some kind. But they are reconstituted notions of ethnicity, of a reactive rather than primordial ethnicity created and changed in processes of accommodation to, or conflict with, the regionally uneven economic integration of the colony's different groups. The legal realm that guided labour and migration, and the technological realm that improved mobility and communication also played parts in influencing spatial perceptions of opportunity among and between African groups and *vis-à-vis* them and the Europeans. In some cases what previously had been considered as minor differences were accentuated; in others, differences were made up from scratch [cf. *Papstein, 1989*]. In short, the very representation of African interaction into an ethnic division of labour and an ethnic ranking was a product of a radically restructured society whose continued existence depended on new institutionalised powers rather than on the particular characteristics of the multiple local groups.

ETHNICITY IN POST-COLONIAL ZAMBIA

Such spatial notions of opportunity may change over time. This has been the case between the colonial period and the present in Zambia, where until recently the one-party state (United National Independence Party) and its government were the power axis around which ethnicity reconstituted itself in a steadily declining economy. Officially, it was 'One Zambia, One Nation', with a count of 73 'tribes', according to *The Tribes of Zambia* [*Brelsford, 1966*], a handbook published by the government printer shortly after independence. The national dance troupe, a group of performers from many regions, presented the 'One Zambia, One Nation', theme at many public functions as did a bevy of women and children hauled away from township markets and schools to fill up the airport and line the streets on the visits of important foreign dignitaries. These women's access to market stalls required them to be members of the party and thus to be 'party militants', a term through which the party reinterpreted Zambia's political history. Of the 73 'tribes', the Lozi had for many years performed a recreated form of the *kuomboka*, the annual move of the *litunga's* barge between flood plains and higher lying areas. Drawing attention from politicians and tourists, this and other recreated traditions of annual rites which had long fallen into disuse, have been staged by other groups throughout the 1980s. For example, the Ngoni, the Lunda, and the Nsenga. When national television features such performances, it conveys one contemporary meaning of ethnicity in Zambia: spectacle.

This kind of ethnicity carried little affective meaning to ordinary people, such as those I have studied in Lusaka for what will soon be a 20-year period. This, I believe, is a product of the kind of work I have undertaken. Had I been a political scientist studying national and regional politics, I might have been able to speak more engagingly about the shadow in the closet, the 'tribalism' scholars label ethnicity and which continues to play a part in who gets what, when and how, in terms of cabinet posts, ministerial offices, parastatal companies, and allocations of loans and project moneys.

When residents of Mtendere, a low-income township on the outskirts of Lusaka where I have conducted my work, compare themselves to other urban Zambians, they do not speak about ethnic specificity, but about difference in opportunity and power. In their descriptions of themselves, they have appropriated the term 'the common man' from the official discourse but with meanings that derive from the difference they perceive between themselves and the *apamwamba* who live in *mayadi*. The Nyanja term, *apamwamba*, means literally, people on the top. In the status terms of post-colonial Zambia, one could say that the *apamwamba* have replaced the colonial *wazungu*, the Europeans, or whites in general, who used to live in 'the yards', that is, the low-density residential areas.

Consider the following characterisation which my long-term assistant, who lives in Mtendere, made after one of her first long-distance trading trips across the border into Zaire in the mid-1980s. 'The Wazungus in Zaire', she said, 'are *Mwenye* (Indian)'. In the Copperbelt region, specific economic opportunities have opened up and disappeared, attracting the involvement of groups of 'foreigners' who have been described differently by their Zambian hosts and their surrounding society. I have already mentioned the Kasai women of the colonial period. After independence, that region has seen the making and scapegoating of so-called Zairians, Senegalese, and 'West Africans'. These are ethnicities that have been redefined during recent history. Their boundaries have been constructed through cross-border interactions and they depend very much on legal issues and the power relations they involve.

People from the eastern province form the largest element of Lusaka's population, and Nyanja, the language of much of the eastern province and Malawi, functions as the lingua franca. Today, you will hear more Bemba spoken in Lusaka than when I began my research there in the early 1970s. This reflects a reorientation in migration patterns, especially in the wake of the decline of the copper mining industry, located in the northern, Bemba-speaking part of the country.

Most of the men in my household sample worked in low-income manual or service-oriented jobs, with no striking ethnic clustering in distinct occupations. Those of their wives, who over the course of my studies have involved themselves in income-generating work, mainly in the informal sector, do not represent some ethnic groups rather than others. Their particularity is age, not ethnicity, and what they share is poverty. Beyond their non-ethnically marked worlds of work and neighbourly interaction, I have observed invocations of ethnicity in a few contexts, although there may be others. One context concerns a grouping with diverse southern African backgrounds (including Sotho, Tswana, Zulu, and 'coloureds') who pool money to relieve funeral expenditures. Sometimes this pooling takes place at a 'subscription party'. The participants refer to each other with the English term 'homeboys'. I see this as a regional association rather than a distinctly marked ethnic group. In addition, both churches, and the party, involve themselves in funeral arrangements.

Another context in which I have seen ethnicity invoked has less to do with organised group activity than with individually staged action. It has to do with the identification of an 'ethnic' specialist on the occasion of a daughter's initiation. In some, but not all, of these urban households such an occasion still involves the young woman in partial seclusion during which a senior woman of eastern province background teaches her the skills and responsibilities of a sexually mature woman. Her teacher is not necessarily from the very ethnic group she herself represents. At times of health crisis, some Mtendere residents also consult skilled persons of distinct regional backgrounds who are considered knowledgeable about non-Western medicine. Ethnicity in these instances does not revolve around sentiments about shared backgrounds, but around specialised knowledge and skills.

My research on domestic service in Zambia has also touched on ethnicity. The division of labour in domestic service draws on gender in that men outnumber women by far and puts men and women to work in different ways with different remunerations. Beyond that, servants are drawn from many different regional groups by the same principles as those that informed servant recruitment during the colonial period: proximity to the opportunity structure in both spatial and temporal terms. Since the economic slow-down of the mid-1970s, domestic service has attracted workers from more varied ethnic backgrounds than in the past. Yet employers of servants, Zambians and expatriates alike, keep repeating the colonial stereotypes concerning which ethnic groups provide better or worse servants. Prospective servants are aware of these distinctions and sometimes fabricate ethnicities in the face of expatriate employers. And Zambians who hire other Zambians to do domestic work do not agree on the significance of ethnicity. Some of the Zambian householders I interviewed said they preferred to hire a servant from their own ethnic group, because such a person would readily understand the way in which things should be done. But some employers took a very different stance. They preferred not to engage people from the same ethnic group as themselves, because a fellow ethnic would understand too much of what was being talked about between husband and wife, and within the household in general [*Hansen, 1989: 231–2*].

The conclusion regarding ethnicity in Zambia that these observations from my own work invite me to draw are of the lukewarm kind: ethnicity is there, and it isn't, which explains why I myself have not found ethnicity to be a very salient relationship in structuring local-level relationships in Lusaka. The axis in this case, as I have suggested, is not ethnicity, but the socio-economic domain which colonial and post-colonial politics have constituted and changed.

ETHNICITY AND GENDER IN ZAMBIA: WHAT KIND OF A RELATIONSHIP?

My general unease about giving much weight to ethnicity as a subject of analysis in Zambia finds a parallel in the juxtaposition of ethnicity and gender. What kind of a relationship are we talking about: a strategic one, or one that is experiential, involving questions about identity and discursive subject positions? Certainly, at the level of group interaction, gender has on occasion been a rallying point in women's demonstrations in Zambia both during the colonial period and after independence. Yet, ethnicity has to my knowledge not played a corresponding part. The potential for an exception was reported to me by a colleague who has done recent research in Lamba villages off the Copperbelt where Senegalese men have married local women. The issue at stake was Lamba women's participation in an ongoing debate about Zambia's gender-biased naturalisation laws.[2] The children of a foreign wife and her Zambian husband are Zambian, whereas the children of a foreign husband and a Zambian woman are not. But in the end, I believe that this issue has more to do with civic rights, and economic access, than it has with ethnicity.

Aside from the observations I have made so far regarding a possible strategic/practical relationship between ethnicity and gender, I am reluctant to go farther and make categorical statements about the relationship between them regarding experience and identity, that is, regarding how people see themselves. My own research focus is on interaction and relationships and regarding them I believe that, concerning them, we can safely say that gender is socially constructed with reference to class, to race, and to a host of other relationships that may include age (or stage in the life cycle), region and religion. It may also be constructed with reference to ethnicity. It has been common within the social sciences to speak of the intersection of such relationships. This formulation warns us against singling out any one of these relationships as the determining one. What we are confroned with in most of our studies is the complex interactions among and between these relationships that are formed historically and that draw on them all, but variously. The safest conclusion then is perhaps to suggest that we cannot understand the interactions of these relationships without reference to gender.

NOTES

1. See Epstein [*1978*] for an exception.
2. Anneke Touwen, personal communication, 30 Jan. 1992.

REFERENCES

Brelsford, Vernon, 1966, *The Tribes of Zambia*, Lusaka: The Government Printer.
Epstein, Arnold L., 1958, *Politics in an Urban African Community*, Manchester: Manchester University Press.
Epstein, Arnold L., 1975, 'Military Organisation and the Pre–Colonial Polity of the Bemba of Zambia', *Man*, Vol.10.
Epstein, Arnold L., 1978, *Ethos and Identity: Three Studies of Ethnicity*, London: Tavistock Publications.
Evans, A. J., 1950, 'The Ila V.D. Campaign', *Rhodes–Livingstone Journal*, No.9.
Ferguson, James, 1990/91, 'Mobile Workers, Modernist Narratives: A Critique of the Historiography of Transition on the Zambian Copperbelt', Part One & Two, *Journal of Southern African Studies*, Vol.16/17.
Gluckman, Max, 1961, 'Anthropological Problems Arising from the African Industrial Revolution, in A. Southall (ed.), *Social Change in Modern Africa*, London: Oxford University Press.
Hansen, Karen Tranberg, 1989, *Distant Companions: Servants and Employers in Zambia, 1900–1985*, Ithaca, NY: Cornell University Press.
Heisler, Helmuth, 1974, *Urbanisation and the Government of Migration*, New York: St. Martin's Press.
Matejko, Alexander, 1976, 'Blacks and White in Zambia', *Ethnicity*, No.3.
Mitchell, J. Clyde, 1987, *Cities, Society, and Social Perception: A Central African Perspective*, Oxford: Clarendon Press.
Mitchell, J. Clyde, 1966, 'Theoretical Orientations in African Urban Studies', in M. Banton (ed.), *The Anthropological Study of Complex Societies*, London: Tavistock Publications.
Mitchell, J. Clyde, 1956, 'The Kalela Dance: Aspects of Social Relationship Among Urban Africans in Northern Rhodesia', *Rhodes-Livingstone Paper No.27*.
Papstein, Robert, 1989, 'The Creation of Ethnicity', in LeRoi Vail (ed.), *The Creation of Tribalism in Southern Africa*, London: James Currey.
Siegel, Brian, 1989, 'The "Wild" and "Lazy" Lamba: Ethnic Stereotypes on the Central African Copperbelt', in LeRoi Vail (ed.), op. cit..

Gender, Ethnicity and Popular Culture in Kenya

BODIL FOLKE FREDERIKSEN

I tell you what, man, ... women are a hopelessly impossible tribe
(George Kamau Muruha, 1972).

POPULAR CULTURE

This study is an attempt to explore a puzzle in contemporary African popular culture. It has arisen from my work on urban culture in Kenya and the form and content of its products, especially popular writing. In that writing, gender relations are widely represented and discussed. Questions of male and female identities and gendered social practices are the very organising principles of much popular culture in Kenya, as elsewhere. Ethnic and racial relations between Asians and Africans are also present, but Kenyan African ethnic identities and practices as an issue of concern to everyday life are absent as a self-conscious theme. Knowing that African ethnicity has been of great concern, both historically and in contemporary Kenya, its apparent absence in popular literature is a puzzle.

Ethnicity may be present, but only at a deeper embedded level. It is not depicted on the front cover of books; it does not thrust itself at the reader the way sex and gender relations do. Serious literature such as the novels by Ngugi wa Thiong'o spring from the historical experience of ethnicity. If popular novels, directed at a much broader audience, articulate ethnicity they do so in circumspect and hidden ways, as I hope to show.

My approach takes for granted that popular culture reflects popular preoccupations in ways which one does not have to be a deconstructionist to unravel; an unfashionable view which uses written material, including fiction, as source material for gaining insight into the social fabric. Another assumption is that popular culture represents issues which are of central concern to ordinary people, and that it does so in ways which are constrained by the political culture of a given society. If that is so, the products of popular culture comprise a valuable collection of data about areas which are not otherwise easy to research.

Bodil Folke Frederiksen, International Development Studies, Roskilde University Centre, Denmark.

The discourses of popular culture articulate the multiplicity of identities of groups and individuals in ways which imaginatively represent their experience of daily life, for instance, the way in which they are constantly engaged in making informed, strategic and cultural choices. These discourses are an element in creating the utopia of the possible. Contested areas of social difference and inequality such as ethnicity and gender may be put on the agenda in ways which in themselves indicate what are the key questions, which are most hotly contested. Their articulation are soundings in deep political waters, but they may not necessarily be put openly on the agenda. Their hidden presence indicates where the lacunae and silences in the political culture of a social formation lie.

I am concerned with modern genres of popular culture. My main category of primary material is English-language novels and magazines.[1] Popular written culture in Kenya from the 1960s to the present day has been predominantly written in English. Although there were attempts by the colonial administration to encourage vernacular writing, and in spite of the fact that Swahili is one of two national languages in Kenya, only literature in English has managed to reach a public wide enough for publishing to be profitable in economic terms. So I have chosen to focus on popular English-language novels and a proliferation of popular magazines. Amongst the latter I have looked particularly at one, *Joe Magazine*, which appeared for a period of five years in Nairobi in the 1970s.[2]

It may be argued that this written culture hardly counts as being 'popular' from a quantitative point of view. It reaches only a limited audience of more educated people, primarily those who are young, live in towns, and have some earning power. Richard Mabala's [*1990*] comments about modern Swahili popular literature in Tanzania are equally true for English language popular literature in Kenya. 'Popular literature reflects and speaks to the rising urban classes. The writers themselves are of and for these classes ... their works express ... the preoccupations and contradictions of those classes.' He suggests that the popular writers are not simply 'an urban phenomenon but in fact ... are representative of the classes of the future' [*ibid.: 30*].

My reasons for using the term 'popular' about this body of written literature have therefore to do with its quality rather than its quantity. It creates a discursive field encompassing areas of popular concern and it addresses an audience which is similar in social composition to that reached by Western popular literature. Furthermore, it is formally close to Western genres like the thriller, the romance, the 'true' confessions of criminals, or the moralistic fable.

Oral culture does not hide ethnicity; it articulates it at many levels. In urban areas the expression of ethnicity has come to take forms that are different from those in the countryside. Language is an important marker of ethnicity; the

switching and shifting between available languages, as examined by David
Parkin in Nairobi in the 1960s, is part of a socio-cultural strategy, aiming at
maximising social space and resources [*Parkin, 1974*]. Ethnicity is fun in
everyday transactions of a non-conflictual kind. It adds spice to life. Ethnicity
is the *way* people do things: it is culture.

The way individuals and groups do things at the present moment is rooted
in cultural practices accumulated over a long span of time: history. And history
is remembered and comes alive as kinship and locality, two powerful ingredients in ethnicity. Genealogy elaborates the surface of oral culture, and immediately marks ethnicity at several levels, so there is a vibrant surface level
articulating and even celebrating ethnicity through greetings, jokes, in negotiations, and in conflicts.

In this respect, written English puts popular novels in a strait-jacket which
means that they cannot compete with oral cultural practice. The novel cannot
represent ethnicity directly, as language use and switching can in verbal
exchanges. The English language evokes only a brief historical memory and
furthermore reflects only areas touched by modernity. A first step has perhaps
been taken towards breaking the taboo on articulating ethnic difference in
popular written culture. Recent writing, particularly by David Maillu, the most
popular and prolific writer in Kenya, is making use of more than one language,
in his case Kikamba, Kiswahili and English. This may be seen as a movement
towards articulating a modern mixed urban identity in which different
dimensions of a person rub and melt together as Swahili prefixes do with
English verb roots: 'mpuzzle', 'kudisclose' and 'anaexpect'.

In Europe an important source of popular writing was class, seen as a basic
category of social difference. However, class conflicts enveloped gender relations and were often the main mechanism defining the plot of novels and
stories: class set the action going. But class in contemporary Kenya is not such
an obvious choice as an organising principle of popular culture, ethnicity is
much more likely to be. Class as lived experience is not pervasive in the urban
centres from which the writing springs; nor are rural conflicts often experienced in terms of class. Social inequality seems to be both experienced and
interpreted according to dimensions other than class.

Popular novels in Kenya conform to a format invented in Europe and the
United States that was present and further developed in Africa from the 1950s.
Speed, action and direct speech are central formal ingredients in both the
European and the African novel. A layer of didacticism is a characteristic
African addition. The contents or the stuff of the novel, however, are wholly
African, as indicated by localised and specified settings, and the naming of
space and characters. The fact that the novel form originated in the West and
in its popular version adhered closely to Western model, does not explain why
Kenyan narratives leave the cultural richness of ethnic difference untapped,

especially when local novels have undergone various other transformations both in content and form.

During the 1960s processes of social change particularly amongst the urban populations, began to put questions of gender high on the agenda and into all areas of popular culture. There was a social energy in questions of gender that could not be contained. The growing economic and social independence of women, particularly in urban areas, was unsettling. Although this tendency probably affected relatively few people at first, it quickly became reflected in popular writing.

Most popular novels are written by men and represent a male-dominated world. Offices, streets and bars are favourite settings. Women are rarely protagonists, but present as wives and girlfriends, located socially in the border area between working women and prostitutes. In these novels being a nurse or a secretary invariably implies sexual availability.

In the few narratives by female writers, women are protagonists. In the widely read narrative poem, *What Does a Man Want?*, a woman expresses her bewilderment with the various and conflicting roles open to contemporary African women:

> My mother says/Win him through his stomach ... My friend's advice might be better ... Charm him, she says/Be fashionable, she goes on:/ Be elegant!/ Be modern! ... Be a good mother to his children/ ... I have a good idea/Auntie comes excitedly/A good hostess may work:/Be a good hostess to his friends/ Charm them! ... Win him through the in-laws/Through the jealous mother-in-law/The most difficult to please/Feed her!/Bluff her!/Cheat her! [*Likimani, 1974: 1–4*].

This narrative explicitly treats relations between an Asian woman and an African man, a white woman and an African man, and an African woman and a white man. African ethnicity is absent.

In popular writing, themes of ethnicity and gender are brought together in a proliferating genre of novels which take African–Asian ethnic and racial relations as a theme. A sub-genre within that literature, which we may call the African–Asian romance, deals with power and love relations between those groups of the Kenyan population.

I Will be your Substitute, by a female writer, Ngurukie [*1984*], is fairly representative. A young African woman tries to make it in the city. She falls in love with an Indian who is the son of the owner of a fashion boutique in River Road. He loves her too. They marry and she becomes co-owner of the shop.

The pattern and narrative sequence are very similar to the standard Western novel format; the difference is that ethnic and racial difference rather than class are the engine of the plot. Ethnicity is where difference and inequality are located and by bringing it out into the open and elaborating it, decisive steps are being taken towards overcoming it.

In these novels ethnicity is dealt with in a progressive or modern way. From initial hostility and the portrayal of the older generations as die-hard ethnic chauvinists, the resolution negotiated mainly by young people is that ethnic issues should be debated, and from a basis of mutual understanding people should then be evaluated and treated in terms of personal merit, not cast in ethnic or racial stereotypes.

Water Under the Bridge, a blockbuster written by an Asian, Dawood [*1991*], is the saga of three dynasties – Asian, African, and European. Oloo, the Luo patriarch, reflects on the difference between his own generation and that of his children: 'He knew the subtle difference between "home" and "house" and the need to return to the soil of his ancestors. All these mores of tribal belief would haunt him if he dumped them like an over-worn suit' [*ibid.: 314*]. Like the white patriarch who dies of aids, and the Indian head of family, who emigrates to Canada, Oloo loses out to the new generation: 'They longed for the romance of breaking old shackles. Not only the shackles of colonialism – these were long broken and forgotten, but the chains of class, tribe and dogma' [*ibid.: 345*]. The inter-ethnic festivities at the marriage of Meena and David is a 'masterpiece of pragmatism', where 'alcohol flowed freely, chicken and mutton were served, only beef had been prohibited. This had been followed by a music party with an Indian troupe from London performing rock-and-roll, jazz and disco music to the tunes of Indian songs' [*ibid.: 345*].

What is being worked out is not only a basis for harmony between different ethnic groups, but also the ideal of romantic love and its precondition, the creation of two independent individuals. In the novels of African–Asian love relations, Asian women are given more social space than are the female characters in novels about Africans. Creating fictions about free Asian women who are culturally unknown, may serve to free the imagination with respect to African women whose constraints are all too well known. The utopia of the love-marriage may be attractive also as a model for inter-African ethnic relations, and it is probably closer to the lived realities among young Africans than those prevalent between Africans and Asians.

When relations with Asians constitute a novel's sub-theme, they are treated in a much less fantastical manner; in a manner more in line, probably, with average African experience. In such novels Asians may only be referred to. A conversation from a popular novel, *A Worm in the Head*, between two African mechanics employed by an Asian is representative: '"I don't like Asians, Fred".' That's Jack telling me. He hates them anyway. I also hate them. The other day, Jack told an Asian foreman at the garage that he would shave him with a screw-driver, if the foreman did not take his pink-pigment from Jack's sight' [*Githae, 1987: 302*]. The two friends dream of opening their own garage: 'We shall employ our own mechanics, some who will be poached from Premji's garage. I cannot stand an Asian telling me when to eat or when to shit and such-like things. I am a grown-up and this is not Delhi or Bombay. This is Nakuru – Kenya! he finishes. I agree with him' [*ibid.: 305*].

The language of nation is intermingled with ethnic concerns such as eating habits and hygiene. And as the discussion develops questions of race become yet another strand in the novel's attempt to understand inequality and power-lessness: 'There was an evident colour and cast discrimination in almost every act that the Asian group at the workshop did. Led by the foreman, the other Asian mechanics were openly prejudiced in each act' [*ibid.*].

A parallel treatment of Asian foremen on a building site may be found in Meja Mwangi's, *Down River Road*, one of the few modern Kenyan novels which treats class difference, and which also fleetingly touches on African eth-nic relations by casting its two protagonists as Luo and Kikuyu.

In popular literature white racism and prejudice is not an important issue. It is treated with less passion and vehemence than African–Asian relations. If whites are present they are mainly the dupes of African prostitutes, or tourists who set different standards for consumption and behaviour and are portrayed in a good-natured, even admiring way. An echo of European ethnicity may be noted in passing, in that in popular gangster novels the arch villain is often German. Indigenous whites, the settler community, are only rarely repre-sented.[4] This may seem surprising in the light of the history of white racism in Kenya and the atrocities committed by whites, or under the command of whites, during the Mau Mau. A dislocation seems to occur, making Asians the target for hostile feelings which are rooted in a history of suppression by whites.

Popular magazines also reflect women's changing roles and new possibili-ties. One fifth of the total number of issues of *Joe Magazine*, which were all organised thematically, had women as their main theme. One issue dealt in some depth with a new marriage bill, another with the status and problems of a female professional group: secretaries. Most of the short stories which fea-tured in the magazine dealt with marriage, infidelity and prostitution.

Although the magazine never debated ethnicity openly, its readers (experts in the area) would be able to decipher the disguised ethnic discourses and styles in the text and illustrations. The 'modern' African/Kenyan personality is jeered at in subtexts in the magazine, as can be seen in this excerpt from a short story, 'A Day in your Life': 'In the sitting room the kids are quarrelling about something. In English of course. They don't speak any other language although you and your wife are Africans. But you are modern Africans.

Modern Africans don't teach their children any other language apart from English' (*Joe Magazine*, Nov. 1973).

GENDER AND ETHNICITY IN KENYA'S POLITICAL CULTURE

I wish to return to the question of why gender can be debated, flaunted and engaged with in popular written culture whereas African ethnicity leads a secret and furtive life, and also to address the reasons for the popularity of the Asian–African theme; another puzzle whose solution may throw some light on the unwillingness both to discuss African ethnicity and to bring together articulations of gender and ethnicity when it comes to Africans. My suggestion is that part of the answer lies in the different histories of gender and ethnic relations in Kenya.

All through colonial and post-independence history, ethnicity has been highly politicised, whereas gender has not. Gender and ethnicity are both elements in a person's identity and thus help demarcate his or her scope for social action. However, while both are socially constructed and situational, they occupy very different spheres in the careers of individuals and in the power play and political culture of a society. Gender is not and never has been a basis for politicisation at the national level in Kenya, whereas ethnicity always has been.

The structural inequality which has emerged on the basis of classifications of race and ethnicity is a consequence of global, regional and local structures of power and divisions of labour, and the reformulation of these structures has posed a threat to hegemonies at all levels. In regions and societies where an elite's hold on power is precarious, as is the case in Kenya, public discussions of ethnic issues are seen as a threat to the national project. They have to be circumspect and disguised.

Gender identity has cross-culturally given rise to social inequalities which have left women with less public and, probably, less private power than men. Socially-based ethnic inequalities have reinforced women's subordination in oppressed ethnic groups, but they may modify or lessen the suppression of women from favoured ethnic groups. The persistence of marked social differences between groups of women is one factor which has historically worked against the politicisation of women as a group. The social and ideological pressures in many societies confining women to private rather than public space is another. The outcome in Kenya is that women do not count as a political factor of importance. Articulation of female identity and gender conflicts do not pose a threat to the hegemony and consequently public debates on gender and sex may be open and direct.

Ethnicity in Kenya is constituted by a long historical narrative. Although informed by pre-colonial times, it reflects more acutely the cleavages of modern Kenyan political history, particularly the Mau Mau and the divisions of power and resources in the decades after 1956. One of the main preoccupations of colonial political culture was ethnicity or tribe. Narratives and categories of ethnicity were a stock-in-trade of colonial official and popular culture, both written and oral. For expertise, the colonial administration relied on diligent District Commissioners who were supposed to gather information on, and be versed in, local language and culture. For them and for the Administration at higher levels, ethnic difference was not only a tool for understanding the foreign surroundings, it was also a policy instrument used as a technique of government in that foreign territory.

During the height of the Mau Mau insurrection, from 1952 to 1954, ethnicity came to be critical. The core members of that insurrection were from the Kikuyu ethnic group, and ethnicity was used by the authorities as the criterion by which people were favoured or persecuted, co-opted or sent to internment camps. Housing for Africans in Nairobi had been segregated along racial lines, but not along ethnic lines, in a planned way before 1952. The subsequent ethnic segregation drew deep lines of division into modern Kenya. One of the important political tasks after Independence, made urgent by the social and moral panic of the Emergency years among both Africans and Europeans, was the discrediting of ethnicity at all levels.

The transition marked by Independence necessitated the construction of different narratives and categories that were more liberating and in line with the nation-state project, and that were better suited to making sense of social problems, and fashion instruments for social control. The state apparatus, which was dominated by the Kikuyu, invoked and made use of a category at the same level as the ethnic group, namely, the nation, so as to make sense of power relations and the distribution of resources.

The eventual victors in the struggle for state power, the KANU Party, discouraged and actively suppressed debates about ethnicity in the run-up to Independence and for a long period afterwards. Ethnicity continued to be present in oral culture, an area that was supremely difficult to control, but was censored out of the written culture. Prevention of debate did not inhibit the allocation of resources along ethnic lines, but may have been thought to disguise it. But, of course, people kept being born in Murang'a, or in Nyanza and kept identifying with their home region when they moved elsewhere. In Kenya, as in other African countries, the notion and practice of having a rural home was important for cultural identification, for political affiliation, and, in the absence of a fully-fledged urban economy, as a welfare and economic resource.

Gender relations belonged to a different problematic and were not politicised by the colonial government. Gender was a deliberately muted category in colonial political culture, given its male-dominated and patriarchal character. The colonial authorities had great difficulties in discovering women, let alone communicating with them. They were generally seen as amorphous relations, adjuncts to men. They became a 'real' problem, calling for action, only when they were without male guardians: as domestic workers, prostitutes, or left behind in rural communities. If women were a problem, it was a problem which African men were expected to handle or, to a much lesser extent, they could become a target for the benevolence of colonial wives.

Given the absence of gender in the colonial culture one might have expected that with Independence gender would become one of the categories that was seen as being most useful and in need of debate, but this did not happen. The discussion of gender was not initiated from above to any significant degree.

Although women's groups were encouraged after Independence, they were mostly conceived in the same mode of benevolent patriarchy as that characteristic of colonial officers.[5] Furthermore, they aimed at social, not political development. Women's problems caught the popular imagination only with the launching of the women's decade at the large conference in Nairobi in 1975, as can be seen from popular novels, newspapers and magazines. The institutional arrangements of that event and the processes which it initiated, meant, however, that women's issues were seen as being put on the agenda by the international rather than the national community.

Asians were an important social group in pre-independence nationalist politics. Their leaders sided mainly with African political leaders in the struggle for Independence, and Asians were better educated and more economically powerful compared to the African majority. However, they were not very visible in post-independence political life and they did not have a strong *public* voice in the political arrangements of Kenya, although they continued to have a central role in the professions, trade and services.

The Asian community is very much present at an everyday level in modern Kenya, particularly in the urban areas. They live physically and economically close to the African urban populations, but still lead separate lives, being different and socially and culturally unknown. There may thus be a need to construct imaginatively the inner life of Asian communities. Everyday conflicts and debates about power, inequality and access to resources are being fought out in the discourse of African–Asian race and ethnicity. Like gender relations, this area is charged with emotion and social energy and can only be contained with difficulty.

The Asian community does not claim a right to the leadership of the nation in the way that African ethnic groups do; nor do women. There is a parallel here with gender relations. The portrayal of Asians and their relations with Africans in popular writing is not seen as a threat to the stability of the political regime, consequently, lack of direct or indirect censorship is another reason for the presence of the theme.

Finally, I wish to suggest that there may yet be another reason for the presence of a discourse handling African–Asian ethnic tensions in popular writing. This discourse, while representing in a straightforward manner lived conflicts between Africans and Asians, may also serve vicariously to debate inter-African ethnic conflicts. Thus conflicts and tensions among Luos and Kikuyus may be displaced and worked out imaginatively.

THE ROLE AND POSSIBILITIES OF POPULAR CULTURE

It is remarkable that even the most hardened ethnic relations, such as those between Asians and Africans in Kenya, may be played with and softened in written popular culture, a realm of relative freedom. It is equally remarkable that questions of sexual practices and morality in their modern, urban versions are openly and even aggressively present in that culture. With the present opening up of the political climate of Kenya there are signs that the ban on issues surrounding human rights and political oppression can no longer be upheld. In the long run, this opening up will also inevitably mean that African ethnicity will come to find its proper place in popular written culture.

In the new political situation in Kenya, where the Kalenjin 'tribe' has been mobilised by the President to destabilise the political processes in the multi–party era, a mobilisation which in its turn activates other 'tribes' as counter-forces, one can argue that ethnicity as a category is primordial and ossified precisely because it has not been open to scrutiny. Buried ethnic feelings and identities exist in a raw form, and are easily available for the most crude politicisation.

If one wants to make sense of ethnicity and gender and assess their role and importance in modern society it is not therefore enough to look at ethnic and gendered *behaviour* as may be observed in the structuring of society, that is, in the division of labour, formation of groups, social movements, political parties. Such behaviour can only be understood once one pays attention to the *history* of social change. And that understanding needs to be based on the interpretation of the long historical narrative, that includes reasonings and emotions that have come to form that behaviour. I wish to suggest that popular culture in a broad sense provides the material which can link private concerns to public action.

NOTES

1. From my experience, corroborated by interviews with writers, publishers and school teachers, English seems to be the language of urban written popular culture. Swahili is being pushed in the educational system, and some Swahili popular novels are being published. Their sales are, however, much lower than that of English language literature. In Tanzania the language of popular literature genres is Swahili but in Kenya the uneven diffusion of the language nationwide, among other factors, has created a different situation.
2. For a fuller treatment of *Joe Magazine*, see Frederiksen [*1991*].
3. 'Untouchable' [*Maillu, 1987*], 'I Will be your Substitute' [*Ngurukie, 1984*], and 'Day After Tomorrow' [*Tejani, 1971*] are some of them.
4. Two recent novels which also deal with the settler community and descendants of settlers may indicate that change is under way. Both 'The Mixers' [*Gicheru, 1991*] and 'Water under the Bridge' [*Dawood, 1991*] are family sagas, recreating the intertwining fortunes of African, Asian, and White families, over several generations.
5. In his programmatic memories, 'Freedom and After', the Kenyan nationalist leader, Tom Mboya, comments approvingly on material prepared in Uganda for the advancement of women. 'I found the tales of Mary Mukasa, the school–teacher's wife, who looked after four young children, kept the house spotless and put on a clean dress before her husband returned home ... both charming and worthwhile' [*Mboya, 1993: 161–2*].

REFERENCES

Dawood, Yusuf K., 1991, *Water under the Bridge*, Nairobi: Longman Kenya.
Frederiksen, Bodil Folke, 1991, '"Joe", the Sweetest Reading in Africa: Documentation and Discussion of a Popular Magazine in Kenya', *African Languages and Cultures*, Vol.4, No.2, pp.135–55.
Gicheru, Mwangi, 1991, *The Mixers*, Nairobi: Longman Kenya.
Githae, Charles K., 1987, *A Worm in the Head*, Nairobi: Heinemann Kenya.
Likimani, Muthoni, 1974, *What Does a Man Want?*, Nairobi: Kenya Literature Bureau.
Mabala, Richard, 1990, 'Popular Literature in Tanzania', paper presented to African Association of Teachers of Languages and Literature, *ATOLL*, Botswana.
Maillu, David G., 1987, *Untouchable*, Nairobi: Maillu Publishing House.
Mboya, Tom, 1993, *Freedom and After*, Nairobi: East African Educational Publishers Ltd.
Mwangi, Meja, 1976, *Going Down River Road*, London: Heinemann Educational Books.
Muruah, George Kamau, 1972, *Never Forgive Father,* Nairobi: Kenya Literature Bureau.
Ngurukie, P.G., 1984, *I Will be your Substitute*, Nairobi: Kenya Literature Bureau.
Parkin, David, 1974, 'Language Shift and Ethnicity in Nairobi: The Speech Community of Kaloleni', in W.H. Whiteley (ed.), *Language in Kenya*, Nairobi: Oxford University Press.
Tejani, Bahadur, 1971, *Day After Tomorrow*, Nairobi: East Africa Literature Bureau.
Watene, Kenneth, 1974, *Sunset on the Manyatta*, Nairobi: East African Publishing House.

Monogamists Sit by the Doorway: Notes on the Construction of Gender, Ethnicity and Rank in Kisii, Western Kenya

PHILIP RAIKES

INTRODUCTION

This analysis looks at the 'common sense' of gender, ethnicity and age-status, and how they are formed in Kisii District, Kenya, a region that has been notorious with respect to sexual violence.[1] I had originally intended to look at various gender issues, in Kisii and 'the West', hoping that interesting comparisons would emerge. They did; but the approach of the two parts diverged, and increasingly so as I proceeded. It is, of course, much easier to see patterns 'over there', than 'here', where the wood cannot be seen for the trees. Apart from that, the discussion of Kisii focuses specifically on the formation of 'normal' gender, age and ethnic constellations, which are all that this outsider was able to observe, while looking at public social life (and engaged in research on agricultural credit). Regarding 'the West', this 'normality' was precisely what the study aimed to question, taking a number of studies from a standpoint transgressive of 'normality' and showing some of the absurd contortions involved in reproducing a 'right-thinking' common sense [*Dubermann et al., 1991; Epstein and Straub, 1991*]. This was difficult to integrate with Kisii, where I found no material of this nature by which to compare.[2]

With regard to Kisii, the approach has been successive 'zeroing in', from a broad, historically-based discussion of context, via discussion of various hypotheses put forward by others, down to an account of a specific event, which demonstrates one way in which common sense notions of gender, ethnicity and age are formed, and which can be seen as a simplified example of the interplay through which a habitus is formed. Since reference to 'habitus' and 'common sense as a cultural system' might lead the reader to expect a heavy theoretical apparatus to the study, I should explain that these are notions which I have found provocative and helpful, without claiming to have built a theoretical analysis, still less a model, upon them. I have used them more or less as below.

Geertz's discussion [*1983*] of 'common sense' or 'plain fact acknowledged by plain men', like Galbraith's 'conventional wisdom' comprises those sets of

Philip Raikes, Centre for Development Research, Copenhagen, Denmark.

beliefs which 'right-thinking' people accept without question, and upon which they base many, if not most, actions and further opinions. As both show, in their respective spheres, much of this consists of a farrago of myths and stereotypes, often mutually inconsistent. Geertz is illuminating on the shifts, contortions and refusals to see what does not fit, by which common sense is reproduced or repatched. The components of common sense have a strong tendency to underpin existing power and status relations, which is hardly surprising since the 'right-thinking men' most active and effective in its propagation are those whose status and respect are reinforced by it.[3] But this is neither simply a matter of the instrumental actions of the powerful to maintain their positions; nor yet just the power-structures of society reproducing themselves 'objectively' and so determining the activities of individuals (who are thus reduced to mere 'bearers' of different external social determinations). It is among the purposes of Bourdieu's [1977] concept of 'habitus' to point up this dual nature of social process as being subject to external determinations, which however are themselves the product of the contextualised decisions of individuals.

The case cited shows common sense about gender, ethnicity and age, being reproduced in a social process which served to emphasise the existing rank-order among those present, even while providing scope for some to improve their relative standing by entertaining the gathering or flattering its leaders. The outcome of such processes is in no sense indeterminate, since the game is played on a field and under rules largely defined by the existing common sense and allocating power and prestige on this basis. This field and rules form the context for what Bourdieu calls the 'logic of practice', and which he contrasts to the formal logic of optimisation theories or game theory. Here decisions and actions do not follow an explicit decision-calculus, but are felt by the actor to be intuitive; to 'come naturally'. No small part of this is a repetitive learning and socialisation process, which combines an unquestioning acceptance of the 'rules of the game', as given by 'tradition'[4] and 'common sense', with the acquisition of virtuosity and 'feel for the game' in the process of playing it. Respect derives not only from the size and status of the part played, but from the virtuosity with which it is played. Although the general tendency of this process is conservative, the fact that actors are following their own implicit strategies, does allow a certain 'degree of freedom' for change. Clearly there is considerable overlap between 'tradition' and 'common sense', so all this is related to the 'invention of tradition' discussed by Hobsbawm and Ranger [1983].

ETHNICITY, GENDER AND AGE IN KISII, KENYA

Kisii is a mountainous district in western Kenya, the home of the Gusii people, of whom there are some one and a half million. It is an area of high rainfall, high soil fertility and the highest rural population density in Kenya. Well over 90 per cent of dwellers in Kisii are Gusii, with rather few living elsewhere, except in the Kenyan capital, Nairobi.

Although Kisii is taken as an example for this study, by the accident that I studied rural credit there, it is in many ways 'made for' a study of ethnic and gender construction. These lie very much on the surface of social relations, not only as a staple of conversation but in the common terms of address which tend to specify gender and age (or stage), and in the case of foreigners, ethnicity. I was more frequently than in other places I have been in East Africa, addressed simply as *Mzungu* ('European', that is white man) and 'foreign' Kenyan Africans were also often addressed and usually referred to in terms of 'tribe'. A neighbouring people, whose forms of address do not discriminate for age and gender, are criticised in Kisii on that account. I should make clear though, that while other external observers confirmed this impression about Kisii, my own other experiences of East African rural areas come largely from Tanzania, where the expression of 'tribal' stereotypes is less common and far less officially approved than in Kenya, reflecting different governmental attitudes, from the early colonial period to the present.

Kisii has a reputation for tension and violence, most especially as concerns gender relations. Rates of murder and rape are said to be among the highest in Kenya, while wife-beating is both common enough and serious enough to be reported by primary health workers as one of the more common causes of women seeking treatment. Yet Kisii is also a place and community which inspires a strong sense of collective identity, both as expressed verbally, and in terms of people feeling homesick when away. Talking to people in Kisii, one is left in no doubt of their self-identification as Gusii, or that Kisii is the centre of the world. Yet in some respects, this 'community' is nothing of the sort, but rather a series of 'bracketed' sub-communities, each in conflict with one another, from the seven major 'tribes' of Kisii, down through clans, sub-clans and lineages to families and their members. Philip and Iona Mayer [*1965: 53*] refer to a society 'organized for overt competition' with 'acknowledged rivalry at every point' and expressed in a 'favourite axiom' that 'brothers fight for the mother's breast'. In short, a highly segmented society, and one in which solidarity within segments seems to an unusual degree dependent upon opposition between them.

Robert and Barbara LeVine, who studied another area in Kisii some eight years later, also found abundant evidence of social conflict though, focusing upon a more 'modern' community, they found wealth to be a major axis.

Wealthy men are respected and poor men despised: indeed, the term for poor man is an insult in the Gusii language ... The wealthy live in fear

of poisoning, witchcraft and sorcery at the hands of their jealous neighbours. (But) this does not inspire the(m) ... to share with others ... On
the contrary they use their wealth to dominate their inferiors through
loans and threats of expensive litigation [*LeVine and LeVine 1966: 11*].

The LeVines also found abundant evidence of gender conflict, both ritualised
and real.

GUSII HISTORY

A first step in considering this combination of strong 'ethnic identity' and the
clash of groups within it, is to consider pre-colonial history. As Ochieng'
[*1974*] shows, the Gusii migrated from the plains to their present mountain
home, as much under pressure from powerful neighbours as from preference.
Once there, they formed an isolated Bantu-speaking enclave, surrounded by
different Nilotic language speakers; Luo to the north and west, Kipsigis and
Maasai to the east and south. Thus, although geographical boundaries were
both shifting and inter-penetrating, linguistic and cultural boundaries would
tend to have been sharper than where speakers of related languages shaded into
one another.[5] Relations between the Gusii and their neighbours – and between
different sub-groups of Gusii – were of a shifting nature and always liable to
be disrupted by cattle-raiding. This was a major means by which patriarchal
family heads added to their wealth, power and prestige, and a part of the
socialisation of young men as warriors, when they were sent out to herd,
defend and raid cattle. Since any group outside the unitary family might be fair
game, this could be seen, very crudely, as the type of strategy which would
generate the segmentary system considered above.

From what evidence there is, it seems that Gusii lived in proximity with
Luos more peacefully than with Maasai or Kipsigis, although expressed levels
of respect would lead one to expect precisely the reverse. The Kipsigis and
Maasai, like the Gusii, circumcise boys and girls, while the Luo do not, which
strongly affects ethnic stereotyping, implying as it does a missing rung in the
age-status ladder.[6] Circumcision is of crucial importance both in the formation
of an age hierarchy and in defining its ideological basis in (for males) manliness. The child being circumcised, usually between 8 and 12 years old, though
previously older, must undergo this very painful procedure without anaesthetic
and under the taunts of a crowd of drunken adults, without tears or the slightest
flinching, on pain of being scorned as a coward and the threat of being
considered a failure for life. There is a sense in which Luos, who do not
undergo this process, are considered by Gusii as never attaining the status of
adults.[7]

But the construction of ethnicity among the Gusii was also, in part, a colonial phenomenon. The colonial incursion itself was an unusually bloody affair, with brutal reprisal raids and huge communal fines in cattle, which impoverished them significantly. After this, labour recruiters were let loose to get labour for plantations and for the 1914–18 wartime Carrier Corps, infamous for a death rate much higher than that of the troops. This they did by bribing colonially appointed chiefs and headmen with drink to deliver men into labour by force [*Gethin, n.d.; Raikes, 1992a*]. The colonial state also set about dividing Kisii from its neighbours, and its population up into sub-divisions, for purposes of law and administration, codifying convenient pieces of 'customary law' (normally a blend of compromises, deals and (mis)understandings) under the far from disinterested control of the Chiefs they had appointed.[8]

With population well under a tenth of its present level, land was not initially in shortage, especially as the cattle population had been severely reduced. However production of crops for sale started during the 1920s and by the 1930s a few chiefly and educated families were beginning to accumulate land. Together with population increase, this began to put pressure on land so that by 1948, Mayer could record that the primary focus of court cases had shifted from livestock to land, also noting an early enthusiasm among the Gusii for law and litigation, which appears to persist. By the 1960s, population density was already among the highest in Kenya, and by now, at over 500 per square kilometre overall, it has reduced farms to pocket-handkerchief size, often composed of long thin strips up and down a hillside.

Ethnic divisions have been further aggravated since Independence, and especially during the reign of Daniel arap Moi, by a politics which specifically plays upon them. The country has been divided into a series of satrapies, corresponding in most cases with ethnic or sub-ethnic boundaries, and placed under the control of leaders whose main, if not sole, qualification has been loyalty to the President. In return for this they are allowed a free hand within their area and a share in the centrally allocated state or donor funds. Not that such decisions are made once and for all. On the contrary, there is a constant jockeying for positions and funds, the gains going to those who are most assiduous and outspoken in asserting their faith to the President and hatred or scorn for his enemies.

Kisii has been affected by this in a number of ways. First, it is a buffer zone between the Kipsigis and Maasai, related and faithful to President Moi, and the Luo, suspect as the base for opposition politicians like the late Oginga Odinga and parties, like FORD Kenya. At the same time, the Gusii are the sixth largest ethnic group in the country, and seen in some senses as a pliable 'swing' group, of Bantu language and culture, but separated, both geographically and politically, from the other main Bantu concentrations in Central-Eastern (Kikuyu, Embu, Meru and Kamba) and Western (Luhya) Provinces respectively. During the period I spent in Kisii, this generated a quite unusually instrumental and non-principled politics. In the first half of 1992, the tensions exploded into serious violence, with attacks on and murders of Luo workers in the tea plantations of the (Kipsigis) Kericho District, but also with riots and deaths at a number of political meetings in Kisii and other parts of western Kenya.

More recent, larger-scale occurrences of ethnic violence have tended to concern Kalenjin/Maasai against Kikuyu and sometimes Luo. But the assertion of ethnic identity by the Gusii and their neighbours is still very much a part, and one of the most destructive and dangerous parts, of modern Kenyan politics. It is also an aspect of politics with strong links to male gender politics, since it is bound up with the ranked hierarchy of patriarchs upon which political control in Kenya is dependent, and expressed in that most manly of activities, fighting.

GENDER RELATIONS AND CONSTRUCTION IN KISII

Whether gender distinctions are sharper among the Gusii than among surrounding peoples I have no means of assessing and find it hard to think of useful categories for such a discrimination. That they are marked by tensions and generative of significant amounts of violence seems clear, though the only statistical evidence I have seen is from the mid-1950s. From this it emerges that there was a specific gender aspect to Gusii violence. While the rate of homicide for Kisii was just above that for the urban USA and 15 to 20 per cent above those for Luo and Kipsigis [*LeVine 1966: 80*],[9] for rape Kisii had about three and a half *times* the rate of the urban USA and respectively twice and two and a half times the rates for Luo and Kipsigis [*ibid.: 87*]. A number of sources have commented on the extent of rape in Kisii; from 1937, when performance of traditional dances at markets was prohibited, because of 'an outbreak of rape' [*ibid.: 64*], to the 1980s and special rules for Peace Corps women working in the District, following the rape of a volunteer. Levels of wife-beating and other intra-household violence are said by health personnel to be very high, this also being reflected in responses to a questionnaire administered to a large random sample of Kisii women [*Raikes, A., 1990*].

Historical factors might account for changes over time in levels of intergender violence, but there is little evidence for this, one way or the other. Comparison with neighbouring peoples seems to indicate something specific to Gusii society. It may be worth considering some hypotheses which have been put forward to explain this.

The simplest, most reductionist, but in some ways most appealing, is *population density*. Kisii has the highest rural population density in Kenya, and the tensions generated by this can be claimed directly to induce the high level of violence (shared, according to 'local knowledge', with Meru, another high population District, with whose people the Gusii feel some affinity, including mutual comprehension of each other's language). But this appears too simple; evidence from the LeVines' 1950s figures is ambiguous, since higher population density in Kisii, is offset by greater pressure on resources in South Nyanza; and the evidence is of high levels of violence, not increases.

Where *propinquity* is concerned, LeVine [*1962*] tested a variant of this thesis; the relation between geographical proximity of (polygamists') co-wives and accusations of witchcraft. Here the underlying assumption was that, because of the effects of the 'house-property complex', co-wives would almost necessarily be rivals, that this would be expressed in witchcraft and witchcraft accusations and that the level or intensity of these would be dependent on physical proximity. The peoples compared are Gusii, Luo (South Nyanza) and Kipsigis. LeVine finds the relationship to hold, with the Gusii intermediate between the Kipsigis, whose co-wives seem often to have lived up to several kilometres apart, with witchcraft accusations significantly fewer, and the Luo, where both the proximity of co-wives and the frequency of accusations was higher, despite the higher crude population density in Kisii. The problem with this calculation is the nature of the information, which is people's and colonial administrators' general impressions about the level of witchcraft, at best an unreliable basis. Moreover it appears that LeVine's fieldwork was confined to Kipsigis and Gusii, leaving the Luo to be characterised by the assertions of their neighbours, uninflected by their own opinions. Since witchcraft accusations are usually aimed at other peoples, this seems a significant source of bias.

The 'house-property complex' does seem worth discussing as a generator of intra-household violence, though not in a comparative sense, since Luo, Kipsigis and Gusii alike are organised on this basis. The basis of this 'complex'[10] is: '[that] all property is owned by men but is allotted by them to their several wives to be transferred eventually to the sons of these wives. This creates within domestic groups, mother–son sub-groups called "houses" which compete with each other for a share of the property' [*LeVine, 1962: 40*]. This is certainly true of the Gusii, where the co-wife relation is recorded by virtually all observers as being especially tense and fraught, though I. Mayer [*1972: 137*] refers to the 'double risk that the wives might quarrel among themselves or ... gang up against the husband'.[11] Of course, the tensions are not simply between co-wives themselves. Probably most of the overt violence deriving from the 'complex' is between the sons of different wives.[12] But while it is clear that the 'house property complex', or the social relations which it represents have a significant effect on the structure of violence, who fights with whom, it is less clear that it need necessarily affect its overall level. In terms of more general relations between men and women it is of crucial importance in severely limiting women's access to land and in directing it through a husband or male children. It is, by the same token, a very important factor contextualising a woman's habitus, both in the sense of what are the components of her 'strategy' and regarding the ways in which she follows it.[13]

One very interesting analysis comes from another paper by Iona Mayer [1975], which looks at data on social classification and distinctions from field-work in Kisii in 1946–48, through a transactional analysis based on and refer-ring to Goffman. In terms of the categories used in this study, one could say that Mayer concentrates on one particular aspect of common sense, that hav-ing to do with social distinction, its formalisation and reproduction. 'People who care about social distinctions have an interest in keeping apart', to which end they employ 'routines of dissociation (which) mark social boundaries and affirm distinctive identities ... The more explicit and systematic are the routines of dissociation ... the harder are the edges of social distinction' [ibid.: 259]. This hard edge is related to traditionalism, and contrasted with the mod-ern northern middle-class 'open bathroom' family. Kisii is taken as an exam-ple of this traditionalism and examples are presented to show the large number of cases in which boundaries are marked and formalised.

Mayer then poses the question: '[as to] how much these ... avoidances ... owed to a generalised preference for clear-cut social types and how much to the vested interests of one particular type. For here above all the special position of men in Gusii society was being affirmed and "'realized"' [ibid.: 263]. Referring to Durkheim on separation as the essence of the sacred, and to Goffman on how 'distancing' helps create or maintain 'the aura of respect', Mayer outlines processes in which routinisation of dissociative rituals reproduces a series of social distinctions, radiating out and down from the patriarch. In doing so, it 'naturalises' them, in the sense of generating the feeling that this is just the natu-ral way things are. However, at the same time it also 'denaturalises' them, in the sense that the distinctions are marked and accentuated by the rituals.

For Mayer then, the maintenance of patriarchal rank is central to a whole series of dissociative rituals and routines which in turn generate a hard-edged common sense about relationships. Clearly the Goffman-derived transactional analysis prefigures part of 'habitus' and of the somewhat looser theoretical approach of the present study.

A very different analysis, which has been used to explain inter-gender vio-lence in Kenya, including Kisii, is 'male loss of identity' under colonialism and in the post-colonial period. Here the argument is that men, dispossessed of their pre-colonial roles and identities as warriors, cattle-raiders/herders and patriarchs are somewhat at a loose end identity-wise. This is seen to be among the reasons for current exaggerated male aggression and anomic violence against women who, by contrast, are seen as having retained all their roles, indeed accumulated a few more, and thus strengthened their identity [Silberschmidt, 1991].

I have a number of problems with this line of thinking. Some of these are conceptual as, for example, the question of whether one can have more or less identity, and so what 'loss of identity' means. Another is whether one can apply a notion developed to cover the problems of individuals, by extension to whole societies, or their male members. A third problem is simply that I am insufficiently clear about what 'male identity' means and how an analysis which is based upon it integrates all the other identities which a given man can have (African, Gusii, Morenda Clan, farmer/businessman/landless, hail-fellow-well-met, mature man of substance, Seventh Day Adventist, and so on), or come to that considers processes whereby certain identities preclude others (that is strict Presbyterian/right-thinking, beer-drinking man). At the very least, if 'male identity loss' is to be seen as a causal factor, this would seem to require discussion of how various identities are formed and interrelate.

Another set of problems relates to the evidence and its interpretation. This argument would seem to propose an increasing level of violence visited by men upon women, while most of the evidence simply shows high levels. There is a certain tendency to assume that former 'patriarchal discipline' has given way to 'anomic violence', but this is largely conjecture, and at that, conjecture based on 'golden age' nostalgia. Moreover, much of what reality there is to the assumption derives from legal changes which have imposed at least formal limits to the control by a patriarch over 'his' womenfolk.

Moreover, the evidence for 'loss of male identity' among Kisii or Kenyan men is much the same as for the argument that colonialism, male labour-migration, cash-cropping and the need to produce food on more limited areas, have unequally increased the labour burden on women, so accounting for observed wide disparities between their heavy work-load and men's considerably lighter one. From this viewpoint, the factors generating 'loss of identity' can be seen as a clear advantage for men, and certainly many of them see it that way. Many men in Kisii regard the hard slog of agricultural labour on their own farms as 'women's work' and demeaning, using this as an excuse for evading it, although some of these will undertake it for wages on the farms of others, which apparently reduces the stigma. But this surely points one towards questioning both the 'naturalness' of such characterisations and the necessity of the supposed loss of male identity. It is also worth noting that, in strong contrast to situations where men feel themselves pushed out of paid work by female competition, not even the most ardent supporters of the notion of male identity-loss have argued that men should assume the functions through which women appear to maintain their identity (weeding crops, washing clothes, collecting water and firewood and staying at home to look after children, for example).

One can also question whether loss of male identity necessarily generates exaggeratedly male behaviour. R. LeVine [1966] has used similar data to draw exactly the opposite conclusion. He compares two different processes deriving from colonial market integration in Africa. In selected Eastern and Southern African societies (one of which is Kisii) labour-migration and limited opportunities for women have increased income and labour-input disparities between men and women. (Men do less farm work than before, but control a larger proportion of product and income.) But in selected southern Nigerian societies, absence of migrant wage-labour and female dominance of local trading has reduced men's control over family income. In this analysis the limited involvement of Eastern African men in agricultural labour is seen as one of the *advantages* accruing to them and in part responsible for their retention of status and control. In this account, it is West African men (or rather those from the specific groups mentioned) who are seen to have 'lost identity' along with relative income and status. Moreover, they respond to this not with exaggeratedly male behaviour but, in this limiting case, the Yoruba, by 'a widespread and intense pre-occupation with impotence' and by a widespread 'occurrence of male transvestism in ritual and cultural fantasy' [*LeVine, 1966: 191*]. I cite this article not to so much push the case it makes as to note the 'heads I win, tails you lose' quality of analyses, in which broadly-defined 'complexes' or identity-crises can as easily be read to generate certain forms of behaviour as their opposites.

A side-light to the above leads into the next series of hypotheses. R. LeVine [*1966*] records Gusii women as 'responding' to their worsened situation by taking it out on their children. Whether this should be seen as a response to a lengthened working day, seems unclear from LeVine's own work. R and B. LeVine spend most of the second half of their book on Kisii [*1966*] documenting and discussing Gusii 'traditional' patterns of child-upbringing, and showing how 'hard' they seem to be. This, and patterns of sexual socialisation do seem to have a significant influence on the observed rigidity of gender ascription and violence of inter-gender behaviour. I should perhaps note that my own – unsystematic – observations only partly bear this out. Evidence of Gusii 'hard' behaviour and child-upbringing are not far to seek, but they are not universal. Despite the enormous status-gaps which divide people of different ages, I saw more adult (peasant) men playing with kids than anywhere else I have been in rural East Africa.

CHILD UPBRINGING AND SEXUAL SOCIALISATION IN KISII

It is dangerous to draw conclusions from evidence regarding child-rearing and sexual socialisation, in the absence of any clear feeling for standards of comparison. The practices outlined here seem very 'hard' to a middle-class northern European, but I have little idea how they compare with those of other peoples, beyond a vague and impressionistic feeling that they are somewhat harder-edged. I should also make clear, as the LeVines do, that their evidence refers, not to Kisii, but to one sub-village in an area of highland Kisii close to the house of the most powerful and authoritative chief the District has ever had. It also refers to the late 1950s.

As might be expected from the very high rate of population growth, both men and women in Kisii set a high value on having many children, though land shortage and the increasing cost of education may have begun to give second thoughts to some (often educated) Gusii, since the period of the LeVines' field-work. For men, a major priority is to have sons, who can inherit their land and continue their line. For women sons are important, both as the means of access to land under the 'house-property complex', and as the means to fulfil the duty of a wife to 'give' her husband sons.[14] Previously this was balanced through bridewealth, in that girls' bridewealth was needed to pay for their brothers' marriages. But for most sections of the Kisii population, bridewealth is paid after many years, if at all. Thus there is a definite preference for boys, while differences in socialisation emerge at a very early age.

Right from infancy, the LeVines describe Gusii child-rearing as 'hard':

> The superior strength of adults and older children is thought to be caused by their experience with cold, which has made their blood firm and resistant. This belief ... may help to account for the relatively little concern Nyansongo parents have about the warmth of naked infants and children on chilly days [*LeVine and LeVine, 1966: 120*].[15]

Breast feeding is at will (when the child cries):

> [but] traditionally Nyansongo infants were fed eleusine gruel from birth, or a few days afterwards, as a supplement to mother's milk. (This) was administered by force feeding: cupping her hand against the infant's lower lip, the mother poured gruel into it and held his nose so that he would have to suck in the gruel in order to inhale [*ibid.: 122*].

However, this practice is said to have fallen into disfavour, partly as a result of mission influence. Again, 'a common way of quieting older infants is to frighten them' by showing them animals and saying that they 'will bite you' if you don't stop crying. They also record that 'the Nyansongo mother does not act very affectionately toward her infant, though other caretakers may do so', the most affectionate being elder siblings and grandparents [*ibid.: 126*]. One general pattern of Kisii child-rearing is that relations are somewhat reserved between adjacent generations, but warmer and less formal between grand-parents and grandchildren. For example, in Kisii, it is grandparents who tell children the names of their genitals, these being not mentioned (still less shown) by parents to children.[16]

Weaning is a sharp and painful process for the infant, and the Gusii word for it ... 'literally means to stamp on, or to step on' [*ibid.: 131*]. Methods include putting bitter substances on the breasts, slapping children and giving them large amounts of solid food. This usually occurs when the mother is pregnant again, and the birth of the new child leads to a fairly abrupt reduction in attention to the older sibling by the mother. 'Often a child does not easily accept the diminution in maternal attention which follows the birth of his younger sibling and severe punishment (often caning) results', in part because the cries of an elder sibling are interpreted as wishing (and so risking to bring about) the death of the infant [*ibid.: 134*]. In general the parental response to the sorts of behaviour one would expect from young children being pushed out by a younger sibling seems to be beating, locking-up and frightening with threats like: 'If you cry, I'll throw you out in the darkness and you'll be eaten by hyenas' [*ibid.: 135*]. Control over defecation starts when children are a bit over two years old and is again based mainly on caning for infractions, though speed and severity of training vary widely. The LeVines conclude that: 'the period between 18 months and 3 years is one of severe punishment for ... infantile dependency behaviour ... our guess is that strong feelings of jealousy and hatred are engendered, but prevented by parental punishment from being expressed' [*ibid.: 137*].

After this, it seems that, if children have learned the various lessons involved, life becomes rather less traumatic, though the mother, according to the LeVines, provides little in the way of emotional nurturance, which comes mainly from grandparents. The main forms of discipline are scolding, caning and, in serious cases, locking out of the house at night, both cold and frightening in view of the stories about hyenas and witches which most children have been told. Young uncircumcised children tend to run in flocks, with the older looking after and disciplining the younger. While there is no hard and fast sexual division of labour, girls are more likely to look after younger children and boys to look after livestock, if any. The LeVines report small groups of children, mainly from the same household. In the more crowded area where I lived, the groups seemed larger and more heterogeneous.[17] The LeVines stress that parental discipline focuses first on respect for adults and modesty in front of them, and then against fighting and sexual play among children. This latter, in their account, already takes the form of aggression by boys and avoidance by girls.

The next major step in life is clitoridectomy for girls and circumcision for boys, which they put at between 8 and 10 for girls and a bit older for boys, though in more recent times the age of circumcision for boys seems to have fallen. In both cases, they record the children, though scared of the coming pain, as being eager to go through this ceremony and reach the more favoured status of young 'adults'. The main differences they record are that girls are held while being cut, while boys have to stand alone without flinching.[18] Boys are also subject to painful hazing afterwards, though the male ceremony is said to be quieter and more serious than that for girls, in which adult women dance and enjoy themselves in a 'loose' manner unthinkable at other times. The main reason cited for girls wishing to undergo clitoridectomy has to do with advancing to adult status. Another related one is to avoid crude sexual harassment from young boys, who are severely punished if found making advances to circumcised girls, and far less so where their younger sisters are concerned.

'From the age of 14 or 15 onward, boys are active in seeking heterosexual affairs, concentrating their efforts, at first on girls in their own community' (unlike marriage, which must be with a woman from another clan). 'Since such ... sex relations ... constitute incest, ... these affairs are extremely surreptitious and fraught with anxiety' [ibid.: 41]. By 17 or 18, so the LeVines were informed, young people were quite frequently sleeping together, though risking severe problems in the event of pregnancy. But 'Nyansongo girls are not frank about their sexual feelings; they feign extreme reluctance even when they will yield quite easily to sexual advances ... (The boy) expects this and enjoys overcoming it, taking pleasure from her protestations and cries of pain'. How very predictable then that 'a youth's mistaking a girl's sincere reluctance for mere pretence can lead to rape, which is very frequent among the Gusii' [ibid.: 43].

It is not uncommon among the peoples of East Africa for marriage to take the form of a stylised abduction, with the bride's relatives chasing the pair and the ceremony involving formal bargaining over the bridewealth to be paid (actually decided upon some time before). In Kisii traditional marriage it was apparently the bride herself who resisted or hid, and the whole ceremony seems to have culminated in a prolonged battle of wills and bodies, she attempting to deny him entry, and he attempting to have intercourse as many times as possible (helped where necessary to hold her down and so on by his brothers and cousins). The '... explicit object of such prodigious feats is to hurt the bride. When a bride is unable to walk on the day following the wedding night, the young men consider the groom "a real man", and he is able to boast of his exploits, particularly the fact that he made her cry' [ibid.: 47–9]. Furthermore, 'the conception of coitus as an act in which a man overcomes the resistance of a women and causes her pain is not limited to the wedding night; it continues to be important in marital relations' [ibid.: 54].

Several aspects of this system seem likely to contribute to increased sexual violence, apart from the obvious brutality of the rape-in-marriage ceremony. The (incest) rules put so many of the available partners for young people out of bounds, as to be almost impossible to comply with. But since compliance with these impossible rules does seem to be considered a necessary condition for decency or propriety, most of the population find themselves in a contradictory situation, which enforces upon them both guilt and surreptitious behaviour. The former, I would argue, tends to be assuaged or taken out on others (men hurt women, women 'deny' men sex), while the surreptitiousness involves the sending of ambiguous or contradictory signals. This on its own would be enough to generate a degree of sexual violence. But in addition, the rules of conduct, strict as they are, do not include (indeed, in their approval of giving pain as right and proper, specifically exclude) concern for giving sexual pleasure to others.

There seems little doubt that there are aspects of Gusii child-rearing and sexual socialisation which could contribute to high levels of violence, especially between the sexes. What this shortened account has not done is to show how by the time they reach adulthood the language and behaviour of men and women has diverged so widely that to a very considerable extent the sexes socialise within their own spheres. Neither does it address change since the 1950s. The marriage ceremony referred to has gone, since it marked the completion of bridewealth. Except for the elite, who are invariably Christians, bridewealth payments are completed, if at all, many years and children after the couple start living together. I also think the 'male pleasure from female pain' picture which emerges from the LeVines' study is oversimplified, at least as applied to present-day Kisii.

AN ENCOUNTER IN THE KISII HOTEL GARDEN

The final section of this study records a personal encounter in which I myself was involved. This is recounted because the form and structure of this encounter was in some ways typical and generative of particular sorts of inter-actions and stereotyped opinions.

Since this involves a story of someone being at least somewhat brusque with me, I should make clear that this was by no means typical of my social relations with others in Kisii and notably in Kisii Hotel gardens. For the most part I encountered a kindness and hospitality which made staying in Kisii a pleasure. Drunkenness is undoubtedly the main precursor to violence, but I encountered the former mainly in its convivial phase and little of the latter. I usually socialised at the Kisii Hotel, the poshest in town and District, where visiting politicians (or one faction of them) stay and drink. After some months I came to see it as having a certain dignity and sophistication and was hurt when friends visiting from Nairobi pronounced the place and my friends as 'very bush'.

The context for the encounter was a major 'dynastic' marriage between children of two important Seventh Day Adventist families in Kisii.[19] Both bride and groom had travelled home from studies in the USA. In his sermon, the officiating pastor made clear that this should be a modern marriage, unsullied by traditional features like polygamy or wife-beating. After the reception was over, a number of the guests repaired to the Kisii Hotel for something a little stronger than soft drinks, and an uncle of the bride, an elderly man of some standing, expressed his utter disgust at the sermon and the (non-Gusii) preacher, for undermining Kisii traditions, like polygamy and wife–beating. A few nights later, the same elderly man was again in the hotel, this time surrounded by a respectful group of younger but middle-aged men. He was clearly eager to return to the same topic and looking for a butt, so it was opportune that a wimpish-looking white man (me) should turn up on the scene. A preliminary warm-up session involved a graphic description of how the pre-colonial Gusii used to drink blood direct from cattle, Maasai-style, described with such gusto that it seemed intended to make me go pale with horror. My polite interest seemed slightly disappointing. But then, warming to the topic, the elderly gentleman, K, said to me: 'You, Mzungu![20] Have you any idea what a good system your people ruined when they stopped polygamy?' 'No'. He continued with a harangue about the superiority of polygamy and polygamists and then another question:

> You, Mzungu! Do you know where monogamists used to sit when people were drinking in the pre-colonial period?
> No.
> Right next to the door – and do you know why?
> No.
> Because if someone came and told him that his wife was sick, he would have to go home and look after the children and cook the food. But your polygamist, if someone came and said it to him, he would just look at him and ask 'Which wife? Whose daughter?' and continue drinking. Knowing, as he would, how women should be ordered, he would be able to tell how serious it was. 'And anyway' (slowing down to let the punchline come through clearly), 'anyway, even if she died there would be someone to cook his dinner!'

This time he genuinely had my mouth hanging open, as the standard chorus of such occasions repeated his last line: 'even if she died there would be someone to cook his dinner!' several times, with gusts of laughter between each one. Collapse of white wimp.

The conversation proceeded, with K in the lead, assisted by others, all eager to tell me what a good system polygamy was; how a polygamist would know how to order or administer a flock of women; how wife-beating was an essential aspect of the social order and a thoroughly healthy phenomenon, bolstered by reminiscences of an American missionary who had come to see the light after some years in Kisii and beat his own wife 'not really hard, just so she ran crying into the yard', and more and more and more.

It would be naïve to read this as simply reflecting the opinions of those present. K was known for sounding-off in traditionalist style and this was taken as an occasion for public re-affirmation of values which few present would have held unambiguously. For one thing, to the best of my knowledge, none of them, K included, was a polygamist. Indeed on another occasion, when he was not present, and nor was any man of his generation, younger men laughed at him for being controlled by his wife. Again, most knew full well (about others if not themselves) that wife-beating is not (and probably never was) an affair of the lordly polygamist majestically dealing out justice, but a much less honourable affair of a man coming home mean drunk and taking it out on his wife and children, or beating the less favourite wife at the instigation of his favourite wife or girlfriend. Moreover, at least some of those present saw their wives as partners on other occasions.

Nor was it just gender dominance which was at stake. This whole mini-drama was structured, as so often, to express the dominance of a senior man (in both age and status) over others. This was expressed in their listening respectfully to his stories, bursting into laughter at his jokes, repeating their punch-lines and never, under any circumstances, disagreeing with him. Such conversations structure not only the relative status of those present, but seem to have a significant effect on the sort of thing which is said, almost invariably more heavily authoritarian and 'male' than would have been the case on other types of social occasion.[21] The significance of this lies (among other things) in the fact that no small proportion of political and other decisions in Kisii and Kenya are taken on such 'informal' occasions, with one or a few 'senior' men in command and apparently under pressure to demonstrate this command by a display of ultra-maleness. So, at the same time as social processes of this nature involve displays of 'feel for the game' (in this case a capacity to lay out the 'common sense' with authority, and to do so with the rhythms and cadences defining a good story) they also both define and are defined by that 'common sense'. Again, while they play a part in defining the authority structure, they are in part defined by it. K would not have been able to speak with such authority without having previously held a political position which allowed him to direct resources towards Kisii and particular persons in it.

This in turn links back to the form of political control in present-day Kenya, which is very much a matter of the delegation of authority from one patriarch to another, starting at the top with President Moi. Obviously this is not all that goes on in the transmission of power, resources and commands in a complex modern state, with the interplay of a variety of different formal hierarchies, and with policy informed by different 'technical' considerations. Certainly these sorts of processes have political dimensions and 'technical' ideologies well worth scrutiny.[22] But I do think that one significant aspect of the whole political process is this ranked hierarchy of patriarchs, each bound to the next up by loyalty and acceptance of authority, often symbolised through encounters in which control by the higher over those beneath is played out. This tends to produce opinions and policies in line with the 'common sense' of right-thinking beer-drinking men, even where this contradicts policies emerging from bureaucratic or 'expert' planning processes. It would be fanciful to take the encounter above as symbolising a whole mode of political control; at most it indicates one type of process among many. I do think though that it points to an aspect of the exercise of political power which is too often ignored, and which needs further study.[23]

NOTES

1. I would like to thank Fiona Wilson and Bodil Folke Frederiksen for helpful comments on earlier drafts. Raikes [1992b] is a longer, more detailed version.
2. LeVine [1966] asserts that homosexuality (and masturbation) are almost unknown in Kisii, which would seem to be borne out by the expressions of disgust and disbelief that anyone could do such things, on the few occasions when I heard the topic mentioned. But this is not uncommon in gatherings of 'normal healthy men' elsewhere, where it is less useful as a measure of the extent of the practices than of the degree of (self) deception in sexual relations, the prevalence of which in Kisii is stressed by LeVine himself (see below).
3. Basic to the male Kisii common sense of gender is the (rightful) dominance of men. Women's common sense is more ambiguous; a dominant viewpoint goes something like: 'stupid, drunken and brutal though he may be, it is still the duty of a proper wife to serve and obey her husband'. Ethnic common sense, as always, puts Kisii at the top, and is suppplemented (sometimes contradicted) by a 'sub-ethnic' common sense that, other things being equal, closer kin or clanspeople are to be preferred and trusted. Concerning age, other things (wealth, education, family status or gender) being equal, youth should always defer to age. In reality, wealth, education and social status frequently 'override' age and closeness of kinship and sometimes even gender.
4. This itself being something which is produced, invented or reproduced [Hobsbawm and Ranger, 1983].
5. One must be cautious not to express this distinction too sharply. There are plenty of cases of individuals or groups shifting between or spanning different 'ethnic' identities, even where their respective languages are very different. There does, for example, seem to have been considerable intermingling of Kisii and Luo, despite major difference in language and culture.
6. The Gusii do not have formal age–grades. But traditionally, young men, after circumcision and before marriage, were sent out to 'cattle villages' (ebisarate), in which they looked after the cattle of their own families and learned to be manly, among other things by raiding the cattle of other families and groups.
7. This is the only explanation I can find for a complaint I once heard from a Gusii about Luos: 'they laugh and joke too much'; that (being uncircumcised) they lack the heavy pomposity deemed 'proper' in a mature man but, thank heavens, often honoured in the breach in Kisii.
8. 'Indirect Rule' is widely assumed to have involved existing 'native' authorities and law. Where, as in Kisii, there had been no previously accepted authorities above the level of the extended family patriarch, 'Chiefs' were often the first opportunists to offer their services to the colonial invaders. 'Customary law' was thus a tradition, if not invented, at least heavily 'interpreted' by them.
9. In the African cases these figures include killings of 'witches', widely thought not to be a crime but rather a great service to the community.

10. A problematic term, whose meaning wavers between simply a group of linked factors and the Freudian, as in 'inferiority' or 'Oedipus complex'.

11. In 'Prisca's Diary', a record of the conversations of a women's group in the early 1980s, collected by the pseudonymous Prisca for Carolyn Barnes, rivalry between co-wives entirely overshadowed 'ganging-up', as topic of discussion and as recorded within the group (largely made up of co-wives). The major point of solidarity between all wives seemed to be their execration of widows, who were seen as a major danger and 'out to get their men' by hook or crook.

12. My fieldwork in Kisii included a relatively small 'block-sample' of some 30 contiguous farm-households. What any questionnaire survey would have shown as by far the largest and richest household, was so rent with quarrels between the sons of co-wives as to have reduced the whole family to a state of misery and the father to having his son arrested and beaten up by the police.

13. Without using the term habitus, this is among the points made in a paper on food strategies in Kisii [Raikes, 1992a].

14. The saddest person I met in Kisii was a woman who had recently been so badly beaten that she could hardly climb into the car when I stopped to give her a lift. Her husband beat her regularly, especially when he had money only for half a skinfull and came home to take her non-existent savings by force. He also blamed her for having borne him three daughters but 'given him no sons'.

15. Nyansongo is the (fictional) name given to the area they studied.

16. An educated Kisii friend told me how being cursed by one's mother was among the worst things which could happen. I asked what this would involve, and he said that the worst of all curses would be if she showed her child her vagina.

17. Perhaps, in part, as a result of 'observer bias', that is that they hung around my gate, waiting for a ride in my car.

18. This difference is of enormous importance in generating different stereotypes. While the female operation is arguably far more painful – and involves a far more serious mutilation (the equivalent of removing a man's glans penis rather than simply the foreskin), only the male operation is seen as requiring and showing proof of bravery. According to Mayer [1972: 129] female 'initiation as a whole was said to teach "sense", whereas clitoridectomy was said to "reduce sexual desire"'.

19. The breakdown of the bridewealth system among most people in Kisii is well documented. Haakansson [1990] shows that among the élite, it has maintained, if not increased, its importance, as a means of excluding 'unsuitable' (non-elite) marriage partners, and of cementing dynastic marriages.

20. 'White man', a somewhat brusque form of address in these circumstances.

21. Thus, one evening, two respectable elderly men regaled an audience of middle–aged men, myself included, with stories of the exploits of a notorious Provincial Commissioner, with a focus on his corrupt use of political power to seduce secondary school girls. On other occasions, both of these men would have expressed disapproval of this sort of thing. Here it was just material for a good laugh and to show the P.C.'s adept use of power. Again the rhythm was of a series of anecdotes leading to a punch-line, repeated to laughter by the chorus.

22. Much of my own work has been concerned with the form(ul)ation of the ideology of agricultural modernisation and the interaction of this, through policy implementation at various stages with agricultural growth. See, for example, Raikes [1988] and references therein.

23. Among other forms for this, I would suggest that it might be interesting to look at one or more of the newspaper columns, like The Daily Nation's Masharubu's World, in which a senior 'beer-drinking man' lays down the law about all and sundry, outlining a very clear patriarchal 'common sense'.

REFERENCES

Bourdieu, P., 1977, *Outline of a Theory of Practice*, Cambridge: Cambridge University Press, 1977.
Dubermann, M.B., Vicinus, M., and G. Chauncey Jr. (eds.), 1991, *Hidden from History*, Harmond-

sworth: Penguin.

Epstein, J. and K. Straub (eds.), 1991, *Body Guards: The Cultural Politics of Gender Ambiguity*, London: Routledge.

Geertz, C., 1983, 'Common Sense as a Cultural System', in *Local Knowledge: Further Essays in Interpretive Anthropology*, New York: Basic Books.

Gethin, R., n.d., 'An Old Settler Remembers', unpublished manuscript autobiography, Rhodes House Library, Oxford.

Haakansson, T., 1990, 'Socioeconomic Stratification & Marriage Payments: Elite Marriage & Bridewealth among the Gusii of Kenya', in M.S. Chaiken and A. Fleuret (eds.), *Social Change & Applied Anthropology*, Boulder, CO and Oxford: Westview.

Hobsbawm, E. and T. Ranger (eds.), 1983, *The Invention of Tradition*, Cambridge: Cambridge University Press.

LeVine, R.A., 1962, 'Witchcraft and Co-Wife Proximity in South Western Kenya', *Ethnology*, Vol.1, No.1, pp.39–45.

LeVine, R.A., 1966, 'Sex Roles and Economic Change in Africa', *Ethnology*, Vol.5, No.2, pp.186–93.

LeVine, R. A. and B. B. LeVine, 1966, *Nyansongo: A Gusii Community in Kenya*, New York: John Wiley.

LeVine, S., 1979, *Mothers and Wives: Gusii Women of East Africa*, Chicago, IL: University of Chicago Press.

Mayer, I., 1972, 'The Gusii of Western Kenya', in A. Molnos (ed.), *Cultural Source Materials for Population Planning in East Africa*, Vol.3, Nairobi: East African Publishing House, pp.122–38.

Mayer, I. 1975, 'The Patriarchal Image: Routine Dissociation in Gusii Families', *African Studies*, Vol.34, No.4, pp.259–81.

Mayer, P., 1949, *The Lineage Principle in Gusii Society*, International African Institute Monograph 24, London: Oxford University Press.

Mayer, P. and I. Mayer, 1965, 'Land Law in the Making (Gusii)', in H. and L. Kuper (eds.), *African Law: Adaptation and Development*, Berkeley, CA: University of California Press.

Ochieng', W. R., 1974, *A Pre–Colonial History of the Gusii of Western Kenya*, Nairobi: East African Literature Bureau.

Orvis, S., 1985, 'Men and Women in a Household Economy: Evidence From Kisii', *IDS Working Paper 432*, Nairobi: Institute of Development Studies.

Raikes, A.M., 1990, 'Pregnancy, Birthing and Family Planning in Kenya: ... A Health Utilization Study in Kisii District', *CDR Research Report No.15*, Copenhagen: Center for Development Research.

Raikes, P.L., 1988, *Modernizing Hunger*, London: James Currey.

Raikes, P.L., 1992a, 'Changing Household Reproduction in Kisii', in P. Kaarsholm (ed.), *Institutions, Culture and Change at Local Community Level*, Occasional Paper No.3, Roskilde: Roskilde University Center, pp.75–102.

Raikes, P. L., 1992b, 'Monogamists sit by the Doorway ... ', *CDR Working Paper 92.7*, Copenhagen: Centre for Development Research.

Silberschmidt, M., 1991, 'Rethinking Men and Gender Relations. An Investigation of Men, their Changing Roles within the Household, and the Implications for Gender Relations in Kisii District, Kenya', *CDR Research Report No.16*, Copenhagen: Centre for Development Research.

Controlled Emancipation:
Women and Hindu Nationalism

THOMAS BLOM HANSEN

In India, processes of economic development, urbanisation and mass education in the last few decades have created a very large group of educated working women, and an even larger group of educated housewives. Furthermore, poor, uneducated women have also become wageearners on an unprecedented scale. These tendencies have served to challenge conventional perceptions of women's room of manoeuvre in the public sphere. They have also begun to erode restrictions on female sexuality and change the ways in which dominant constructions of femininity are imposed upon, and internalised by, women in different social locations.

The growing visibility of women in the public realm has proved to be a pertinent question for the Hindu nationalist movement in India.[1] On the one hand, erosion of the joint family system and the growing visibility and assertiveness of women in the public realm have troubled large segments of the urban middle classes. The Hindu nationalist forces have discovered a considerable constituency for their programme of cultural revival and purification amongst these groups who are seeking security and respectability in a rapidly changing social world. On the other hand, women's quest for greater emancipation and visibility has proved to be a growing challenge within the Hindu nationalist movement itself.

In this study, I wish to argue that the Hindu nationalist movement in India has tried to confront women's quest for a greater visibility and autonomy in the public realm through a strategy of *controlled emancipation*. This strategy, I argue, is derived from the more general attempt on part of the Hindu nationalist movement to cope with modernity through recourse to various types of ideological and physical control. In the analysis, I identify two Hindu nationalist strategies regarding women: one asserts the primacy of motherhood with respect to women's position in society; the other attempts to suture gender conflicts through the controlled emancipation of women under the protective canopy of Hindu nationalist organisation.

Thomas Blom Hansen, Roskilde University, Roskilde, Denmark.

WOMEN IN THE HINDU NATIONALIST MOVEMENT

Hindu nationalism, as with other forms of cultural nationalism, is constituted by a fundamental ambivalence *vis-à-vis* modernity. It is a way of coping with modernity. This means that the Hindu nationalists, like the German founders of cultural nationalism (Herder, Fichte and others), try to overcome the perceived dangers of fragmentation in a challenging modern world, and to live a full and meaningful life, by (re)constructing national genius and cultural roots so they can act as the basis for social life. Like many ethnic movements, cultural nationalism seeks to make sense of the world by constructing one homogeneous culture, and recognise one people as the core of the nation. Cultural nationalism in this sense can be seen as a politicised subspecies in the larger category of ethnicity, that is, where claims of community are made on the basis of an imputed shared culture.

The belief that the community shares a single national culture is central to cultural nationalism; so also is the idea that this popular community needs to be constantly rejuvenated and strengthened in order to prevent its dissolution at the hands of modernising forces. Cultural nationalism seeks to link the ultimate fate, Death, inextricably to the nation and does so by making national loyalty the ultimate and unquestionable identity of an individual citizen and expressing this through the rites and discourse of patriotic sacrifice. It seeks to suture and negotiate the discrepancy between modernity imagined as a state of strength, security and plenitude and the actual painful experiences of loss and conflict that have accompanied processes of modernisation.

One corollary of cultural nationalism's obsession with control is discipline and tight corporate organisational structure. Another is the emphasis on *physical strength and self control:* the ability to control one's desires and libido, and to sublimate these urges through an unconditional dedication and service to an elevated cause.

One of the most striking embodiments of this classic cultural nationalist design can be found in contemporary India. This is the *Rashtriya Swayamsevak Sangh* (RSS) (the National Volunteer Organisation), a tightly organised and disciplined organisation that started in Western India in 1925. Today, it has around two million activists based in thousands of branches all over the country. The organisation is the central body within a vast network of organisations and branches, of which the largest and most prominent are India's second largest party, *Bharatiya Janata Party* (BJP) and the revivalist organisation *Vishwa Hindu Parishad* (VHP), the World Hindu Federation. This entire conglomeration has been the prime mover behind the recent surge of Hindu nationalism. The cohesion and discipline of the RSS is premised on a simple device, the *shakha*, a ritual performed simultaneously throughout the country. Every evening 40 to 50 men, dressed in khaki shorts, meet at a training ground and perform a series of physical exercises and martial training with long sticks (*lathis*). After training they gather in front of a large map of *Akhanda Bharat* (pre-partition India), in assembly halls decorated with images of the god Ram, saffron flags, and a statue of the founder of the organisation. Here, they collectively recite a patriotic prayer in the ancient Sanskrit language, promising life-long selfless service to the regeneration of a pure Hindu Nation, while standing in rows with their hands stretched in front of their chests in a form of military salute.

The RSS and its associate organisations have, from the outset, sought to 'recreate the pride and self-confidence of Hindu culture, humiliated through a millenium by Muslim invaders and colonialism'.[2] In RSS cosmology, Muslims constitute the gravest danger to Hindu culture, and the greatest obstacle for the development of a modern Hindu nation. The large Muslim minority in India (130 million) is demonised as the 'Other', the disloyal, antinational element threatening the fabric of the nation; while Pakistan and other Muslim countries are accused constantly of hatching conspiracies against India. The discourse concerning the recuperation of cultural values has found many takers in the middle class; but in its populist form, the discourse centres on the fears, stereotypes and prejudices regarding the Muslim minority and has provided a mass base for the many different organisations in the RSS family.

Although the RSS family of organisations[3] overwhelmingly organise men, a women's wing, the *Rashtriya Sevika Samiti* (Patriotic Association of Voluntary Women) has been in existence since 1936. Its activities are similar to those of the RSS: physical training including martial exercises; *samskars*, that is moral teachings on the duties and obligations of women, emphasising their role as mothers and caretakers of the family; and *baudhik* sessions imparting Hindu nationalist ideology to the volunteers, the *Rashtrasevikas*. Another vital aspect of the organisation is the building of informal networks among women, extending mutual assistance and help in relation to family problems, childraising, and so on.

According to the 'Founding Myth' of the *Sevika Samiti*, the two founder women were disturbed by the general unrest in the country during the 1930s, particularly by the assertiveness of the Muslims and by the inability of Hindu men to defend Hindu women. The myth revolves around a single incident in which a young newly-wed bride was raped by bandits in a train in front of her husband who, like the other passengers, did not dare to resist the bandits.[4] Given the weakness of the Hindu men (or Hindu society, as it is euphemistically referred to in the *Sevika Samiti* discourse) in the face of Muslim aggression and British domination, women felt they had to learn how to defend themselves physically and morally. It was decided not to incorporate women directly in the RSS, as presumably this would create confusion within the organisation. According to Mrs Apte, one of the founding members, the main argument used was that since men and women are different, have different physical capabilities and occupy different positions in social life, it was better to establish a separate women's organisation. Mrs Apte formulated the RSS view on gender in the following manner:

> ... the reason behind this is that a woman is one half of society and the man the other. For example, an eagle, as long as his wings are balanced he will be able to fly in the sky. If one wing is slightly damaged he will be unable to fly ... We are not asking for the same rights as men, but we should be strong enough to keep this balance ... then society will be stronger, everybody will be more generous and feel compassion for all and work for all, irrespective of caste, class and creed, but be a Hindu and a believer in Hindutva (Hinduness, TBH). Thus the bird will be able to rise up high ... We consider the woman to be the navigator of the chariot of life. The man steers/drives, whereas the woman navigates.[5]

Besides creating practical problems of etiquette and appropriate conduct, the direct inclusion of women would also have violated one of the fundamental theses of the RSS: the creation of a brotherhood of men held together by affection among peers and superiors, and based on the sublimation of sexual energy to patriotic devotion and work. Hence, the *Sevika Samiti* was organised as a parallel organisation to the RSS, as a sort of 'character building' organisation for women. It consisted primarily of wives, daughters and relatives of RSS men and maintained very close relations with RSS at the level of ideology, informal networks and hierarchies. In the early decades of its existence, *Sevika Samiti* worked as an auxiliary force of the RSS, consolidating its overall strategy of creating the new Hindu nation as an alternative civil society. A central task for the *Sevika Samiti* in this venture was to ensure that the children and youth of RSS families continued to be loyal members of the larger RSS family.[6]

STRATEGIES OF 'CONTROLLED EMANCIPATION'

Women's emancipation as a discourse and social practice constitutes a dominant problem for the Hindu nationalist movement. To the older generation of both men and women in the RSS and *Sevika Samiti*, images of the independent and sexually sovereign Western woman condense all the evils of Western modernity. Her independence breaks up family life, and she is, ultimately, rendered unhappy, lonely and abandoned by all.[7] The challenge facing the *Sevika Samiti* is to combine and strike a balance between motherhood and nationhood: on the one hand, *Sevika Samiti* encourages women's participation in civic life, and urges them to become active *national citizens*; on the other hand, the organisation emphasises the primacy of motherhood, and seeks to prevent women's access to education and careers from developing into a desire for individual independence and emancipation, which has become common among younger women in the metropolitan cities in India.

The response of the RSS family to this challenge is a strategy of controlled emancipation. This strategy takes two main forms: (1) recruitment and reconstruction of motherhood in the nationalist discourse, and (2) establishment of an internal institutional patriarchy within the Hindu nationalist movement itself.

Recruitment of Motherhood in the Nationalist Discourse

The *Sevika Samiti* maintains throughout that motherhood (and the concomitant responsibility for family affairs and child raising) is the primary *duty* of all women. What at first glance seems to be a mere repetition of a traditionalist discourse on motherhood is, however, articulated as a set of duties derived from a cultural nationalist discourse. Being a mother and looking after the family lies at the core of national life, and of the reproduction of cultural values in Hindu culture. Women's performance in the public sphere should not be an impediment to motherhood. Education and work must be encouraged but should, simultaneously, be adapted and subordinated to the supreme goal of motherhood, whose rationale is derived from the nationalist discourse: raising children as patriotic citizens in the nation state as defined by Hindu culture.

This construction reflects the confluence of the two rather different currents which have inspired RSS's ideology and organisation. One current was conservative cultural nationalism nurtured in the Western world from the time of its foundation in Germany, based on the institution of the family, and seeing the woman in her role as mother as the ultimate line of defence against the disruptive, immoral forces of modernity. Historically, this discourse has been articulated by Christian Democratic parties in the Western hemisphere, by Central European fascism, by Spanish Falangism, and by the moral majority forces in contemporary USA.

Another current was the nationalist legacy inherited from the nineteenth century cultural renaissance in Bengal. In the latter part of the nineteenth century, the fertile intellectual environment made up by an emerging nationalist, indigenous 'parallel' civil society in Calcutta's middle classes, constructed a narrative on Indian history and culture which became 'common sense' knowledge in the twentieth century. As Partha Chatterjee [*1993: 131*] has pointed out in a recent work, this also included the construction of gender: ' ... the specific ideological form in which we know the "Indian Woman"... is undeniably a product of the development of a dominant middle class culture coeval with the era of nationalism'.

This construct, Chatterjee argues, was shaped under the peculiar circumstances of colonialism. The emergent nationalism made itself possible by bifurcating the social world into an external, material domain where the colonial power (the West) reigned supreme, and an inner, spiritual domain where the indigenous cultural tradition (the East) was superior. The external world, in which the males had to move, was one of immorality, impurity, erosion of the moral fabric, that is, modernisation/westernisation. The inner world, the home, religion, the family, was exclusively Indian and feminine, that is pure, virtuous, and essentially spiritual. In this new nationalist construction of a modernised and 'classicised' culture, from where the popular elements had been purged, the woman was constructed as a goddess, and as an upholder of tradition. But the 'new Woman' of the nationalist era was also enlightened, educated and disciplined, unlike the earlier generations of ignorant women, or the common lower class women who were 'coarse, vulgar, loud, quarrelsome, devoid of superior moral sense, sexually promiscuous, subjected to brutal physical oppression by males' [*Chatterjee, 1993: 127*].

These two inspirations, the family as a bulwark against modernity and the construction of a modern nationalist femininity, were synthesized in the idea of *patriotic motherhood*. This comes out clearly in a collection of articles and speeches by the founder of *Sevika Samiti* [*Kelkar, 1971*]. Three themes run through her writings. First, women are first and foremost *mothers*. To be a good mother, to nurture the family, raise the children and serve the husband is the supreme duty of any woman. Second, motherhood is a supremely patriotic role, as women have upheld the traditional values of Hindu culture during one thousand years of foreign domination. Third, such patriotism does not entail that women must leave the house for reasons of education or work. On the contrary, the best way to serve the nation is to develop one's skills and dedication as a mother and to take pride in preserving the family. Education makes women forget their true duties, and makes them individualistic and self-centred. It dissolves families and places, so that ultimately, women are left in a deplorable situation as 'wage earning servants', 'objects of male desire', and imprisoned in 'mental slavery'. Forgetting oneself, discovering the pleasure of giving and serving rather than receiving, nurturing the virtues of forgiving and compassion, and putting the service of the nation above all else are the main themes in the ideology of the *Sevika Samiti*.

Like the other branches of the network of Hindu nationalist organisations, the *Sevika Samiti* attempts to go beyond its middle class 'cocoon' and mobilise poor and lower caste groups through various social welfare schemes. It is indicative of the condescending and socially conservative view of the women in *Sevika Samiti* that they are imbued with a commitment to instil 'cultured habits' in lower caste groups, in order to make them 'become more aware, assertive and independent in their own way'. In fact, the upholding of caste and class barriers and continued domination by Brahmins are far more pronounced features of the women's wing of the RSS family, compared to many of the other Hindu nationalist front organisations, striving to popularise themselves.[8] This can, I believe, be explained by the obsession of the RSS and its high caste constituency with the protection of women (perceived as more vulnerable) against pollution of all kinds: caste pollution, moral pollution, pollution by excessive public exposure, and worst of all, pollution by contacts with males from other communities, for example, Muslims. Brahmin women, the argument goes, are best protected from pollution by birth; and by virtue of their education and nationalist devotion they are most capable of upholding women's chastity and purity, and are therefore the natural leaders of the *Sevika Samiti*. The control of an immoral modernity cannot, it seems, yet be left to non-Brahmins, still regarded as culturally less advanced.

Recruiting New Mothers

The *Sevika Samiti* leaders openly admit that recruitment of younger members is a major problem. The younger generation of women is either preoccupied with careers and education, or devotes all its energy to the nuclear family; a lifestyle which the older leadership disapprovingly call the 'mummy and daddy culture of modern families'. Although the *Sevika Samiti* has adopted a system of full-time workers and has become more public, the older dominant section of the leadership has serious doubts about the future role of women in the Indian society. They doubt the ability of the *Sevika Samiti* to stem what they see as unhealthy trends of 'self-centred consumerism', of 'depletion of family values', and of the deplorable impact of television. To this older generation, motherhood remains the supreme role and duty of women, a position of unsurpassed 'moulding power' and influence, if carried out dutifully and in accordance with national traditions. The road to gender equality goes through the performance of maternal duties rather than through career and individual emancipation:

> We are not saying that our husbands should start cooking always. But it depends upon us to make them realise that even they can do this work. If we don't then it is our mistake. Everything is in the woman's hand. She can influence her family and give them the right direction. Thus, she can become independent by performing her duties ... Family responsibilities are most important to a Hindu woman. The Hindu tradition asks for it and it is genetically present. We do not endorse old age homes, day-care centres, children moving away from the family, nor divorce.[8]

In a branch of the *Sevika Samiti* in Thane City, an industrial suburb in the Bombay region, the problem of recruitment of young girls is even more acute than in provincial and higher caste environments as in provincial cities like Pune. The problem is how to keep the girls attached to the organisation when they reach adolescence and start higher education. While many children are attracted to the *Sevika Samiti*, only those who come from families with a long-standing affiliation to the RSS remain attached to the organisation when they reach their teens. Others join affiliated organisations, but the 'Bombay culture' is difficult to cope with:

> Although *Samiti* members or sympathisers bring their daughters to the organisation it is difficult to keep them attached if their friends attend other clubs, etc. Our society has become lethargic and the people do not want any discipline. Our camps are always held on holidays and nobody wants to get up early to attend these camps. Nobody wants to take any hardship and discipline ... Now we have to adjust our timings according to the TV programmes. We have started to hold *shakha* from 4 to 6 pm so that the girls can go back in time for their favourite programme.[10]

The steep rise in real estate prices in Bombay's metropolitan economy have affected the *Samiti's* work among women in various ways. The expensive apartments make joint family living increasingly difficult, as only a very few families can afford big apartments. More and more young families live on their own, and more and more women have jobs. This gives women little time and it is harder for them to leave their house after work, the Sevikas explain. Some of the older *Sevikas* also complain that the breakdown of joint families prevents the older generation from inculcating good values and traditions in their grandchildren. They also find that their own children are not very keen on looking after their parents. Those living with a son and daughter-in-law, find it increasingly difficult to get along 'as emotional attachments in families are getting weaker'. Interestingly, the younger working women in the organisation did not regard these transformations of the family structure as a major problem.[11]

CONSTRUCTING AN INSTITUTIONAL PATRIARCHY

The RSS family is a kind of 'political sect', a conservative, yet reformist subculture, in which the individual can live her full life in a sort of extended, societal family [*Jaffrelot, 1988: 829–50*]. The family metaphor and its concomitant elements of integration, emotional bonds, attachment, consensus rather than conflict, and undisputed hierarchy, pervades the entire RSS discourse.

Women's work outside the home, especially education and social work are encouraged by *Sevika Samiti*, but is also embraced and controlled by the many RSS front organisations in the workplace, in the campus, in the social field, in the religious field and in politics. Transgressions of the normal limits of women's activities, such as travelling around the country, going on demonstrations, postponing marriage for the sake of work, are only tolerated *as long as they take place within the RSS family itself.* Women can be full-time workers for the *Sevika Samiti,* if they are looked after by decent and suitable families (of the RSS) wherever the women are sent. Women can go to demonstrations and even camp in the open if this is done under the auspices and control of the RSS. And girls can marry late because of work or prestigious education as long as they are loyal to the RSS.

There are, however, two exceptions to the limited role assigned to women within the RSS family of organisations. In the student organisation, *Akhil Bharatiya Vidyarthi Parishad* (ABVP), the Undivided India Students Organisation, young educated women are gradually questioning the legitimacy of the internal institutional patriarchy in the RSS. According to the organisation, 30 to 40 per cent of its members are girls, and a good number of the girls are activists or travelling much of the time around the country. The ABVP is the branch of the RSS where the transformation of gender relations is most visible, and the place where young women opting for a professional career are negotiating the moral, physical and social room of manoeuvre between career prospects, parents and the peer group/surrogate family of the ABVP. The strategy of the ABVP in this respect seems to be to contain and control this expanding room of manoeuvre by offering, on the one hand, a certain protected space for 'experiments with gender equality' within the organisational framework proper, while, on the other hand, discouraging the girls from challenging the authority of parents, joint family system, the traditional arranged marriage, prospective husbands, and so on. The young women in the ABVP obviously attempt to combine and accommodate these conflicting pulls without transgressing the conventions on female chastity and decency:

> The ABVP policy is that the sex of a person is never considered. Everybody is always told that women should know technical things and men should be able to cook. The leaders always insist that everybody should be able to do all the basic work ... but we are aware of our limits and do not wish to emulate the boys or do all that they are doing like staying in the office after 8.30, moving around at night, sticking posters. ... We do not believe in communication through physical contact, and we never indulge in public display of affections ... in the RSS everyone is taught to respect women, to be friendly but within limits.[12]

However, the notion of the primacy of motherhood (over career) promoted by RSS and the *Sevika Samiti,* is not openly contested. Instead, the girls differentiate between the students' world (play) and the adult world (responsibility):

> We have spoken from our students' point of view, they (*Sevika Samiti*) from a responsible adults' point of view. We endorse this totally. Every woman is more attached to her house than the man. We are always taught to maintain these attachments. We are never encouraged to leave anything to follow ABVP ... Today a woman needs to work. But the work need not be to earn alone. But if the family does not need the money, then there is no need for her to work to earn.[13]

Hence, the contradictions between career and family, between the public and the private, remain unresolved in the lives of the girls. They want a career, not out of material compulsions (like poor women), but as an option. They want to work and be independent and respected, but at the same time they endorse the joint family system, oppose day care centres, and believe that women should sacrifice some years of their lives for the children. They believe in the free choice of marriage partners, but do not oppose arranged marriages. In other words, ABVP is a place where some of these tensions can be played out *under the canopy of the organisational work and a playful student world*, without challenging the fundamental moral and social structures in which the girls' lives are immersed.

The other exception is the militant outfit, *Durga Vahini* (Durga's Batallion),[14] which specifically recruits young girls to undertake more dangerous and physically demanding tasks of militant activism, including prospective confrontations with the demonised Muslim enemy. The main activities are karate classes, *lathi* training and ideological training. *Durga Vahini* aims at organising young girls from poorer and lower caste families, but like other front organisations of the RSS, it is built around a core group of young girls drawn from families with long-standing affiliations with the RSS and Sevika Samiti. One leader described the aim and strategy of the Durga Vahini in the following way:

> The main motive behind the *Durga Vahini* is physical training. Only if we have strength can we have a say in society. We have decided to emphasise physical strength in *Durga Vahini*. ... The motive behind this organization is to strengthen Hindu society and not religious awakening. ... Such organisations are also important to keep the younger generation occupied and to prevent them from falling prey to narcotics.[15]

According to some activists, the response among lower caste groups not previously acquainted with the RSS, is far greater than among better-off upper and middle class families, who, it is said, care little for patriotic issues, and are more interested in entertainment and pursuing their careers. In line with the general paternalistic spirit of the RSS, the organisers are convinced that the *Durga Vahini* will become very popular among lower caste families because of the latent desire among these 'hitherto unenlightened sections' to have (upper caste) cultural values and high culture inculcated in the girls and their families through the encounter with the RSS.[16]

To the RSS the sanctity and protection of the female body from public exposure and physical danger is, obviously, less important in the case of lower caste women. While middle class and high caste women are controlled primarily through morality and ideology, lower caste women (more bodies than minds) are controlled and disciplined primarily through physical exercises.

As I have argued already in the case of *Sevika Samiti*, women's education and access to the public sphere are encouraged, in so far as this does not question the fundamental structures of power and authority within society, and even less within the RSS family. Women in the RSS can do anything, except assert their individuality, challenge the wish of their families, have lovers or extramarital affairs, *as long as it takes place within the RSS*. Women's activities outside the extended family are regarded as dangerous, uncultured, indecent and immoral.

The RSS has thus constructed itself as an 'institutional patriarchy', to whom families otherwise anxious to control and delimit the outward activities of their daughters and wives, can entrust the chastity and purity of their womanfolk.

CAN EMANCIPATION BE CONTROLLED?

The processes of modernisation and discourses of equality have eroded older patriarchal forms in India and given birth to slow, but ostensibly irreversible processes of emancipation among women, lower caste communities and other hitherto marginalised groups in Indian society. These trends accelerated in the 1980s and disgruntled sections of the middle classes, as well as poor but upwardly mobile groups, attracted to the Hindu nationalist promise of fullness, discipline, purity and a 'controlled modernity'. RSS has systematically organised and institutionalised an embryonic parallel civil society in large parts of India. In accordance with the nineteenth century idea of the 'new woman', the feminine space in this parallel civil society is the inner, spiritual domain, that is, the family and the household. But in this construction lies probably also the historical weakness of the entire RSS project of cultural nationalist revival. It is stuck in nineteenth century images of national glory, the strong centralised state, and miltary strength. Sociologically, it is stuck in a sort of 'middle class cocoon', whose upper caste values in the longer run will probably prevent it from striking deeper roots in the still more assertive popular constituencies of lower caste and low income groups, always excluded from the nationalist rejuvenation of Hindu culture.

RSS also appears to be losing the battle regarding gender relations. Younger working women who have acquired a measure of independence in the public sphere are unlikely to give this up in favour of patriotic motherhood and maintenance of the joint family system. It is also doubtful that the institutional patriarchy of the RSS and its strategies of 'controlled emancipation' in the long run can retain its attractiveness *vis-à-vis* younger urban women. It is noteworthy that of all the organisations in the RSS family, the Sevika Samiti has been the least successful during the broad wave of Hindu nationalism in later years. The decisive momentum of this wave has been premised on a systematic campaign that seeks to reactivate the latent prejudices and fears of a Muslim menace. The discourse of 'communal populism' appears, simply, to be the only popular idiom which the RSS family has really been able to master.

NOTES

1. The information and interviews upon which the following argument is built, were collected during almost one year of fieldwork in the state of Maharashtra in India during 1992–93. The argument put forward in this analysis is developed more fully and in greater empirical detail in my doctoral dissertation, *The Saffron Wave*, Roskilde University, 1994 (forthcoming). All interviews and texts in Marathi and Hindi were translated into English by my assistant in Pune, Maharashtra, Ms Urmila Budhkar. I wish to thank Fiona Wilson and Bodil Folke Frederiksen for comments on earlier drafts of this study.
2. Interview with Shripathy Shastri, the RSS chief in the state of Maharashtra in Western India, 5 Aug. 1992.
3. The RSS usually calls its network of organisation the RSS family (*Sangh Parivar*), consciously evoking connotations of warmth, security and emotional attachment beyond ideology and reasoning. The family metaphor is central and highly operational as an instrument of recruitment and cohesion for the movement, which offers a sort of surrogate family to the activists. The family metaphor also refers to the authoritarian and paternalist authority structure which operates within the movement.
4. Interview with founder-member, Mrs Saraswatibai Apte, in Pune, 4 Sept. 1993.
5. *Ibid.*
6. According to a reliable source the regular membership of the *Sevika Samiti* is approximately 100,000, while the number of sympathisers is four to five times larger [*Sarkar, 1993*].
7. This was a version of the predicament of the Western woman which I was confronted with on innumerable occasions during my study of Hindu nationalist organisations. The real culprits in this narrative were Western men who, according to this line of reasoning, displayed a lack of respect for women, letting them become humiliated objects of male desire.
8. This trend is discussed in more detail in Hansen [*1993: 2270-72*].
9. Interview with *Sevika Samiti* activists in the city headquarters, Pune, Bharat Bhavan, 19 Dec. 1992.
10. *Sevika Samiti* activist in Thane, 25 Nov. 1992.
11. Group interview with Sevikas in Thane at the Jijamata Trust during a weekly meeting in Jan. 1993.
12. Interview with female ABVP activists in Pune, 11 Jan. 1993.
13. *Ibid.*
14. *Durga* is a powerful, protective mother goddess, engaging in violent combat against the evil. *Durga* is especially popular in Eastern India.
15. Interview with Mrs R. Bapat, in Thane, 25 Nov. 1992.

16. Interview with *Durga Vahini* activists, in Thane, 18 Jan. 1993.

REFERENCES

Anderson, Walter and Shridar Damle, 1987, *Brotherhood in Saffron*, Boulder, CO: Westview Press.
Basu, Tapan *et al.*, 1993, *Khaki Shorts and Saffron Flags*, Hyderabad: Orient Longman.
Chatterjee, Partha, 1993, *The Nation and Its Fragments*, Princeton, NJ: Princeton University Press.
Curran, J.A., 1951, *Militant Hinduism in Indian Politics: A Study of RSS*, New York: Institute of Pacific Relations.
Hansen, Thomas Blom, 1993, 'RSS and the Popularization of Hindutva', *Economic and Political Weekly*, Vol.XXVII, No.43.
Jaffrelot, Christophe, 1993, 'Hindu Nationalism: Strategic Syncretism and Ideology Building', *Economic and Political Weekly*, Vol.XXVIII, Nos.12–13.
Jaffrelot, Christophe, 1988, 'La Place de l'etat dans l'ideologie Nationaliste Hindoue', *Revue Française Politique*, Vol.39, No.6, pp.829–50.
Kelkar, L., 1971, *Amrit Bundi (Drops of Nectar)*, Pune.
Pandey, Gyan, 1991, 'Hindus and Others: The Militant Hindu Construction', *Economic and Political Weekly*, Vol.XXVI, No.52.
Sarkar, Tanika, 1993, 'Rastriya Sevika Samiti', in Tapan Basu *et al.* [1993].
Sarkar, Tanika, 1991, 'The Woman as a Communal Subject: Rastrasevika Samiti and Ram Janmabhoomi Movement', *Economic and Political Weekly*, Vol.XXVI, No.35.

One Step Backward, Two Steps Forward: The Establishment of 'Tribal' Women's Co-operatives in Bankura District, West Bengal

NEIL WEBSTER

India emerged from colonialism as a multinational and multi-ethnic country with a secular state and a democratic federal constitution and, despite intermittent crises, these have survived to the present day. Setting aside the current crises in Kashmir and the Punjab, the different linguistic, ethnic, and religious communities have been successful in negotiating their existences at the federal rather than national level and the country has not been 'Balkanised' as some had expected at the time of Independence. However one ethnic group has consistently remained outside the politico-cultural mainstream in India, those who have come to be known as tribals. In eastern India they call themselves Adivasis.

Adivasi is a counter-identity to that of being a tribal. It is part of a challenge to the cultural stereotypes that prevail concerning non-Hindu 'tribals' and it helps to generate solidarity in confronting the biased treatment experienced in daily life. But can a consciousness of ethnic or indigenous oppression and rights become linked with a greater consciousness of gender oppression and of women's rights?

In my current research project on grassroots production co-operatives in West Bengal, I have carried out fieldwork in an area where Adivasi (that is, 'tribal') women, in this case Santalis and Bhumijas, have identified a need to organise collectively their own women's production cooperatives. What I want to discuss is the extent to which these can be described as being the outcome of the women's experience of ethnic racism and, if there is a connection, whether it is a straight transfer of consciousness from ethnic to gender awareness or whether it is, as I believe, more subtle in that the female experience of the ethnic condition has facilitated a re-interpretation of the women's gender condition within their own communities.

Neil Webster, Centre for Development Research, Copenhagen, Denmark. Special thanks are necessary to the women of the co-operatives and the workers from the Centre for Women's Development Studies, both in New Delhi and in Jhillimilli, Bankura District, and to Narayan Banerjee in particular.

The terminology is difficult because with both possibilities, I do not want to imply a possible causality between the ethnic dimension and gender-based action. What I do want to suggest, however, is the possibility that the practices and the wealth of accumulated knowledge, both conscious and subconscious, that are generated by one set of social relations (for example, ethnicity) can have consequences for the generation of new practices because of a re-evaluation of roles and experiences located in another set of social relations (for example, gender). Hence the use of the term 'facilitate'. I am also aware that this is only one case and it is always dangerous to generalise in the search for lessons applicable elsewhere.

THE ETHNIC DIMENSION

(1) Being Tribal: The Perception of the State

It was only in the eighteenth century that *jana* (tribe) and *jati* (castes) came to mark a significant division in colonial Indian society [*Ghosh, 1991; Ray, 1972*]. The concept of tribe was institutionalised by the colonial state. Tribals belonged to 'aboriginal races'; the tribal was a 'natural child', a Caliban. For example, the Santal 'may be described as naturally a brave but shy child of the jungle - simple, truthful, honest and industrious - before he is brought into contact with alien influences and taught to cheat, lie and steal' [*O'Malley, 1908: 58 and 72*]. In 1935 the Government of India Act began to classify tribes as 'backward' in order to protect them, giving the tribal juridical status as a primitive and backward person requiring help to become civilised. Post-colonial India has merely continued the colonial policy and its ideology. Today, to be listed as a Scheduled Tribe under Article 342 is crucial for access to reserved employment and other development programmes.

Accordingly, for the state, Santalis, Bhumijas, Lodia, and other tribal communities might have separate identities, but they are all tribal, backward, economic under-achievers, and any cultural uniqueness based on their separate identities is of secondary importance.

(2) Being Tribal: The Perception of the Hindu Mainstream

If the social and economic marginalisation of Adivasis was institutionalised by the colonial authorities, their exclusion was always actively supported by the mainstream Hindu community. The constant need for different caste and sub-caste (*jati*) communities to locate and assert their various claims within the hierarchy of the caste system resulted in Adivasis being placed not merely at the bottom of the social order, but outside of it. Adivasis are regarded as dirty and polluting, in their food, their eating habits, their drinking, their personal hygiene, and much more. They remain beyond the Hindu pale culturally and often physically. Inter-household co-operation between Adivasis and Hindus is quite rare, although it varies from region to region; inter-marriage is non-existent, however. Adivasis are usually allowed to live only beyond the perimeter of a Hindu village, if at all nearby, and segregation is generally practised quite openly. For example, when travelling by bus through Hindu areas, Adivasis are usually required to sit on the floor; they cannot take tea or food within the roadside tea shops but sit at an acceptable distance. In these ways separation and social order is sustained.

Tribals are a source of agricultural labour, a means to clear land, and possible sharecroppers. However, the fact that they do not possess their own entitlements can be seen in their general failure to receive ownership of land distributed under land reforms, in their lack of access to village councils, and the fact that they are outside the *jajmani* system of reciprocal services between the different village sub-castes and their various higher-caste patrons.

In this way it can be seen that both the state's view and that of mainstream Brahmanical Bengali Hinduism imprison the 'tribal' in an assumed traditional past. Locked in the past, they have little claim on the present or the future.

(3) Being Tribal: The Perception of the Adivasi

The key point here is that Adivasis do not perceive of themselves as tribals, but as Santalis, Bhumijas,[1] and so on. In so far as they have been given a generic name, they have in turn rejected it and taken another – Adivasi. They have clear separate identities which have been 'culturised' in their institutions, ceremonies and significations.

Bhumijas (literally 'sons of the soil') were at one time the local rulers in Bankura until colonial expansion and the imposition of Bengali Hindus eventually reduced the majority of them to landless labourers, tenants or marginal landowners. Along with other local 'tribals', they were called '*chuar*', that is 'unclean jungle robber'. For their part Santalis migrated into the area as they sought forests to work in and wasteland to bring under cultivation. Subsequently they became poor tenants or were evicted by the landlords.[2] Despite their similar economic condition, due to their respective pasts, the Bhumijas regard themselves as above the Santalis, a fact reflected in their greater use of Hindu religious and caste practices and the claim of some to be a Scheduled Caste despite their Scheduled Tribal status. Mahatos, the third but smaller ethnic group also found in the area, appear to have originally been close to the Santalis in that they retain certain Santali ceremonies, notably their death ceremony and the payment of a bride price. Today, however they are neither registered as a Scheduled Tribe or as a Scheduled Caste and possess a clearly visible and separate identity; one that is reflected in their dominant role in local political institutions in the area.

A 'tribal' region such as that of south-west Bankura is, therefore, a highly heterogeneous area with clear spatial and cultural divisions between the resident Santalis, Bhumijas and Mahatos. If we add to these inter-community dimensions, the intra-community heterogeneity based upon factors such as land ownership and access to political goods, employment, and of course gender, then it should be clear that the ethnic question of what it is to be Adivasi cannot be answered merely by conceptualising a particular community as a discrete and separate social entity in relation to those other communities that surround it. This would be to take only half of the equation into account. While Adivasis do possess a uniqueness located in their own practices, one must recognise that these are not unchanging primordial characteristics. If these characteristics have a distinct and permanent ethnic dimension, and our normative involvement in identifying them is acknowledged, it is because more powerful social forces have monopolised opportunities, institutions, access to the means of producing wealth and markets for goods and services (economic, political, cultural) that might have permitted the heterogeneous elements within that society to develop in other, possibly diverse and fragmentary, ways. Instead the process that has occurred around them has for the most part reinforced the appearance of 'otherness', of homogeneous cultural strengths and resistance, a separate identity.

With the image of 'otherness' presenting itself and being presented so strongly, it is hardly surprising that the divisions within Adivasi society tend to be underemphasised, and relations that might generate other forms of social action apart from those that reproduce or assert the community's ethnic identity are unexplored. Thus gender is examined with respect to the practices that locate women within the household, the kinship group, the village, and thereby reproduce the community. Gender is not examined in terms of the contradictions that it gives rise to.

THE MIGRATION EXPERIENCE

The land retained by the large majority of Santalis and Bhumijas is, for the most part, poor highland reclaimed from wasteland that was once covered by forest. This land is capable of supporting a single monsoon-rainfed crop of rice of poor quality and low yield. Few households possess more than two acres of cultivatable land, and the decline in traditional forest occupations, based on the exploitation of natural resources has meant that migration in search of alternative incomes has become a common practice. Each year several thousand men, women and children from the area migrate to seek work as agricultural labourers in the labour-deficit districts of Burdwan and Hooghly on the gangetic plains to the east. Since the 1960s, the introduction of high-yielding varieties of rice and improved irrigation in the gangetic plains has enabled double cropping. As a result, agricultural labourers migrate from Bankura and elsewhere up to four times a year and for periods of three to four weeks.

The main work undertaken by these labourers is the transplanting and harvesting of paddy. These are both tasks that are traditionally seen as women's work. Women are believed to be more adept and more easily supervised. Moreover, their daily wage is lower than that paid for male labour in the fields.

During the migration period, it is customary that some members of an Adivasi household remain in their own village in order to look after the household's land and cattle. Usually male or elderly members of the family stay behind. Frequently migrating women will be accompanied by their young children if no other woman from the household (an elderly woman or younger sister) remains behind. A typical migrant work group will be between 15 and 25 in number, and mainly female. It is usually led by a man from the village from which the group originates. Sometimes a group will be recruited in advance either by cultivators coming from the gangetic plains or by sending a message to a gang leader. Otherwise gangs will set off with no pre-arranged contract, but will move from village to village in search of work.

The women describe the migration as going on '*namal*' (a journey to the plains). The plains in question are populated predominantly by Bengali Hindus, with the larger cultivators who recruit the migrant labourers usually being from the higher caste Brahmin or Uggra Khatriya communities. While employed in the villages in the plains, the migrant labourers remain in their own groups, living in straw shelters constructed next to the employer's courtyard. Part of their payment is in kind in the form of food, fuel, cooking oil, *biddis* (locally produced cigarettes) and, occasionally for the men, country liquor. With the money earned during migration, shop debts are cleared, pawned utensils are recovered, rice and other loans are repaid, and various ceremonies are financed.

THE FEMALE PERCEPTION OF THE MIGRATION

Local government and development officials have often expressed the belief that migration offered the Adivasis a taste of high living in the more developed regions and that it was therefore popular, especially with the women and children. However, in 1980, a 'Reorientation Camp for Migrant Women Agricultural Labourers' was organised in the locality by the Left Front Government of West Bengal. Here a very different perception of the migration was presented by the migrant women labourers:

> Their main grievance was against the forest policy of the Government. For the tribal women, forests provided the basic means of livelihood. They used to collect free of cost fruits, flowers or leaves of Mahua, Peasal, Kendu and other trees ... But during the last three decades, gradually their customary rights have been abrogated. They were harassed, prosecuted, insulted - and above all were deprived of their supplemental income from the forests [*Bandyopadhyay, 1980*].

Migrant women described how before they left they would be indebted with loans taken at 10 per cent interest per month, and how they had to take further loans or an advance to finance the four-day journey to the work area. While working in the plains they would receive payment in kind each day, but the cash element of the wage was paid only on completing the contract. They could be sacked on the spot and they faced regular sexual harassment from their employers as well as from migrant male labourers who had been provided with crude country alcohol by the employers. Meanwhile, their own houses and lands suffered from neglect; their children had no access to schooling while away or to the traditional knowledge of forest lore and skills. Eviction and desertion of wives and children by husbands had increased, as had wife-beating. The women's traditional recourse to the tribal council and the *Manjhi* or headman was becoming ineffective as their influence over younger men declined. For women, the migratory experience was almost completely a negative one.

This kind of experience was not unique to these women, but the opportunity to present their views directly to a Government Minister (Benoy Krishna Chowdhury, the West Bengal Land Minister), who was committed ideologically to improving the condition of the rural poor, was. He, in turn, handed a list of the women's demands over to a non-govermental organisation (NGO) similarly committed to facilitating the development of women from the rural poor, but with the comment:

> I will see that the government supports all possible follow up action. But the bureaucracy lacks imagination. You do your research right here, and tell us what can be done. These women are ready to organize, (they had said so during the camp), but they will need help. They have trained themselves to live with despair from childhood. They will need time to convince themselves that change is possible ... Money can only be a catalyst, not an agent of change. Change takes place when people's acceptance of a new idea transforms it into a movement. Unless people move, no change is possible [*Vina Mazumdar, 1989*].

It was on this basis that from 1981 a number of tribal women's co-operatives were established in the area. Today there are 17, with a total membership of over 1,800. What is interesting is that the spread of these co-operatives has been through women, not through the NGO or government. Women spread the idea as they moved through marriage and settlement in a new village and during migration as they worked alongside women from other villages. Women have taken the initiative and have come to the NGO asking for help to establish a co-operative in their village.

While various production activities have been attempted based upon traditional forest occupations, the most successful activity has been the establishment of tree plantations for the rearing of tassar silk cocoons. All the co-operatives are now involved in this. The most advanced rear three cocoon crops annually on a total of around 300 acres. The cocoons are sold to the government's silk purchasing body, at the market price, and used in the production of silk.

The co-operatives provide periodic work throughout the year. Each co-operative divides its members into work teams. Each work team works on a shift basis carrying out the various jobs required in each rearing cycle. In the case of many members, the month might be divided into three parts with work for six teams. In some cases the seasons themselves are allocated so that a woman will have co-operative work in one season and none in another. The allocation of work is made by each co-operative society. While most of the women involved still migrate, the number of migrations has been reduced for many women from four to two times a year, and fewer women migrate from a single household at any one time.

The important point to be made here is that the women had identified the problems they faced not so much in terms of the general condition of being Adivasi, but in terms of the more specific condition of being female Adivasis. They were able to turn the effects of ethnic racism and gender sexism into a strength, with the support of the state and the NGO.

The following would appear to be the key facilitating aspects of the migratory experience for the Adivasi women involved. First, the migration required and resulted in a loosening of the ties confining the Santal and Bhumij women to the traditional social space of the household, kinship group, village and community and the subsumption of the female identity which their position within these involved.

Second, it intensified gender oppression through exposure to sexual harassment while away on migration, and at home through an increase in violence against women, in the evictions and desertions of women and children by husbands, and the loss of economic and sexual security these involved.

Third, the migration and all that it involves brought an accumulation of knowledge for the Adivasi women, particularly in how to organise themselves for work, how to negotiate with (male) outsiders over contracts and prices, and generally how to manage their lives in different settings and locations.

Finally, it was an important collectively shared female experience. To this migratory experience and the knowledge it generated, one must add the traditional knowledge of forest work and specifically cocoon cultivation, the knowledge of how to work wasteland, and the experience of the many forms of female cooperation practised outside agricultural work and, of course, the experience of sexism both inside and outside of the boundaries of the household, village and ethnic community.

One particular group of women stands out at the moment. Women who bear the brunt of sexism are unmarried and deserted women who are left economically dependent on a father or brother. In common with other women they are denied land, but the pressure to migrate is far greater and the single woman is expected to accept the status of mistress if it comes with a roof over her head. These women have emerged as the leading activists in this particular co-operative movement. As one woman summed up her experience, 'We have land registered in our names, we have some work, we have many things that we did not have before. We also have many new problems both in organising the co-operative and in our relations with men in the village, but I live for the co-operative now, otherwise I would have nothing' (Interview with Balika Sardar, Peripathar Mohilla Samiti Secretary).

To return to the question of linkage between ethnic consciousness and gender consciousness, although it is dangerous to generalise on the basis of one case, the example of these Adivasi women's co-operatives does illustrate how ethnic relations and gender relations interact when they become the dominant relations affecting certain social groups' everyday experiences. It reveals the possibilities that lie in a situation in which there is an overlaying of ethnic and gender relations and in which the consequences of one set of relations, that is, the outcomes that these give rise to, intensify the relations and outcomes located in the other set.

The concepts of gender and ethnicity are certainly analytically vital because, in the absence of social mobilisation in one of these dimensions (for example where there is no women's co-operative in an Adivasi village), one might easily neglect or underestimate the extent or transformative potential present in the gender relations and structures in that particular community.

At the level of perception by the actors involved, the two are often blurred. The Bengali Hindu cultivator sees the woman, first, as a cheap Adivasi worker, and secondly as a sex object; the Adivasi men see the Adivasi woman during migration as a co-worker, a co-Adivasi and as a sex object; while at home she is a Santal or Bhumij, a mother, a wife, a worker and income earner; if deserted or single she is often seen as a sex object.

It is a question of context and relationship. But in this case women have mobilised on the basis of being female and that is the guide. I would suggest that the process can only be understood if we recognise that the ethnic experience of migration and the accompanying racism and sexism provide a source of lessons and knowledge that allow other questions and ideas to be raised and understood in new ways: a conscious development of a female identity that in turn supports mobilisation in a co-operative movement.

The response of the Adivasi men to this new development is not yet clearly formulated. It may reinforce their ethnic identity as part of an attempt to re-impose their economic and social domination over these 'independent' women.

To conclude, where ethnicity and gender should be linked is in the mind of the investigator. When one asks questions about ethnicity, it is important not to let one's focus and the methodology adopted turn one away from examining other structuring relations and the possible transfer of knowledge and practices between these that might be present within the community under investigation. This is to treat ethnicity and gender not as islands of analysis, but as particular processes and developments that, while crucial in their own right, need to be located within a still greater process of development, namely, the gradual and uneven penetration of capitalism in rural areas and the unintended and often unexpected consequences that this gives rise to. In this the Adivasi women's co-operatives stand out as a remarkable development in rural West Bengal.

NOTES

1. 'Tribals' constitute 5.7 per cent of West Bengal's population. Among tribals, Bhumij constitute 6.7 per cent and Santals 54.3 per cent.
2. In the late nineteenth and early twentieth centuries, Santals never called themselves as such but used the word *Kharwar*, a variation of *Hor*, meaning man. The name Santal probably comes from the area of Midnapore known as Saont, from which they migrated in the seventeenth and eighteenth centuries.

REFERENCES

Bandyopadhyay, D., 1980, 'Travails of Tribal Women', *Mainstream*, Vol.18, No.42.
Ghosh, A., 1991, 'The Stricture of Structure, or the Appropriation of Anthropological Theory', *Review*, Vol.14, No.1.
Mazumdar, Vina, 1989, 'Peasant Women Organise for Empowerment: The Bankura Experiment', *CWDS Occasional Paper No.13*, New Delhi: CWDS
O'Malley, D.S.E., 1908, *Bankura, Bengal District Gazetteers*, Calcutta: Bengal Secretariat Book Department.
Ray, N., 1972, 'Introductory Address', in K.S. Singh (ed.), *Tribal Situation in India*, Simla: Indian Institute of Advanced Studies.

Roots, Routes and Transnational Attractions: Dominican Migration, Gender and Cultural Change

NINNA NYBERG SØRENSEN

INTRODUCTION

The scale and character of contemporary migration is forcing researchers to rethink their assumptions and ideas about migration. Migratory 'moves' cannot be understood as a one-way process where people make a permanent shift from one place to another and gradually lose their accents. Instead, many migrants have transnationalised their existence in the sense that they either move back and forth between two or more countries and/or establish social networks that transcend national borders. When 'poor' countries, like the Dominican Republic and many other so-called Third World nations, can no longer guarantee their population's social and economic survival, people (more or less forced or voluntarily) migrate. By doing this, they may create new global identities for themselves that are superimposed upon the national and local, class, gender, racial and ethnic identities already possessed. Thus the changes implied in migration are neither simple nor unidirectional.

This analysis is a contribution to the understanding of a particular migration process, namely, that of the Dominican migration towards New York City. Out of a population of approximately 6.5 million in the Dominican Republic, an estimated 500,000 to one million are thought to reside in the United States, being highly concentrated in New York City. In recent years, some 15 to 20 per cent of the total population is involved in international migration. It is widely believed, however, though currently disputed [*Grasmuck and Pessar, 1991*], that the Dominican migration stream is dominated by women. Single women often migrate 'on their own' while married women and women living in stable free unions may initiate the migration process. Dominican women are therefore not just wives of male migrants or secondary 'movers' but migrants in their own right. As Morokvasic [*1984*] states, 'birds of passage are also women'. Through an analysis of the relationship between gender and cultural change in migration, of women and men, their interpretations of each other and *their* notions of cultural change, I shall reflect upon whether ethnicity and culture are experienced equally by women and men? My analysis of Dominican

Ninna Nyberg Sørensen, Centre for Development Research, Copenhagen, Denmark.

migration rests on the assumption that overall changes in identities and cultural practices can be read from changes in gender relations. All communities differ in the intricate ways women and men relate to each other; in the way gender is constructed culturally and in the way gender relations constitute a dynamic of a given society. Cultural constructions of gender are symbolic and have strong moral overtones; they are ascriptive, culturally relative and, very importantly, they possess the potential for change [*Gilmore, 1990*]. The focus on migrants' identity and the importance given to gender mean that identity must be understood as intersecting and multi-layered. The concept of cultural identity, an all-embracing notion, needs to be unpacked.

Traditional migration research has primarily approached the movements of people from rural to urban areas and the processes of acculturation, assimilation and/or integration by which migrants are absorbed into the cities of the receiving society. In this scholarly tradition, migration is viewed as an essentially one-way process, in geographic as well as cultural terms, as a linear process from 'traditional' to 'modern', from stability to change. Migrants abandon an underdeveloped periphery that lacks almost everything except culture. When the migrant arrives to her destination she 'carries' culture, not only *with* her (in suitcases filled with tradition) but also *within* her (as an inner pathological condition). Thus, migrant culture is basically viewed as primary relations of kinship, family, and traditional bases of social solidarity. In the migration process individuals gain freedom from former relations of social control at the expense of intimacy. Concomitantly, migrants suffer a *disorganisation of personality.*

Like national identity, cultural identity was conceived, from the point of view of the Chicago sociologists, as something existing in national soil. Migrants became subjected to a kind of 'botanical thought' in which 'broken and dangling roots' predominated [*Malkki, 1992*]. Owing to nationalistic 'natural' notions of a correspondence between geographic and cultural 'maps' and, by consequence, a correspondence between physical worlds and socio-cultural realities, human mobility across boundaries was, and to a large extent still is, viewed as a condition causing disorientation and insanity.

Migrants' loss of bodily connection to their national homelands is still viewed as involving an inevitable loss of morale and emotional bearings [*Malkki, 1992*]. A loss of morale is certainly attributed to Dominicans living in New York City by the surrounding dominant society. But, as will be seen, loss of morale is also frequently debated *inside* the Dominican migrant community abroad and on the island. In these debates loss of morale is placed on the same footing as loss of ethnicity and is very often discussed in terms of gender. This means that not only social scientists but also real living migrants construct the world in which they live and act by drawing on 'botanical' concepts, at least when talking about 'others', see also Sørensen [*1991*].

From this it is evident that the cultural concept in conventional migration research has been defined through boundaries and it has been regarded as 'normal' or as the 'unmarked phenomenon' to stay put within these boundaries. (For a more thorough critique, see Malkki [*1992*] and Carnegie [*1987*]). Consequently, migration has been regarded as a threat to culture since boundaries become slippery when people no longer dwell inside the boundaries of their 'cultural' surroundings. The 'myth of cultural integration', the romantic idea that cultures are consistent, harmonious, and balanced systems shared by people who live and act within the territorial boundaries of a culture, have precluded any theory of cultural change springing from internal dynamics and have left out the role of power in cultural processes [*Archer, 1985*]. That change springs from external dynamics (that cultural change must be brought about by cultural contact) has, on the other hand, been the logic of the myth [*Stepputat, 1992: 7*]. What is really missing is a critique of the confusion of culture with 'the national order of things'. If we, for example, question the 'sedentarist' way of thinking, embedded in theories of culture as well as of migration, we may end up with an understanding of movement and mobility as a historically integrated part of culture that discloses the fixing of specific groups of people to bounded territories as imposed by colonial or national politics of space and power. Further, we may explode the dualistic myth of female immobility in domestic private space/male mobility in international public space.

However, conventional migration theory fails to do so. Accordingly, migrants' reluctance to change (their traditional and sedentarist culture) is seen as either *the problem*, hindering integration in the city, or as affecting an individual migrant's well-being. The receiving society, on the other hand, has everything except culture and is therefore, by definition, modern. Upward social mobility is treated as being at odds with the retention of a distinctive cultural identity in mainstream approaches. As Rosaldo puts it: '...one achieves full citizenship in the nation state by becoming a culturally blank slate' [*Rosaldo, 1989: 201*].[1] As Schwartz further underlines, by treating immigrant culture as *the problem*, researchers have seen ethnicity, tradition, and cultural background as hindrances for integration, thereby preventing themselves from 'discovering creative potential in the meeting between different cultures' [*Schwartz, 1990: 48*]. However, to the extent that migrants are perceived as 'moving targets' [*Malkki, 1992*] or 'emigres-bullets' [*Borneman, 1986*], some sense of *national culture* must exist in the receiving society. How else could xenophobic fears of penetration lead to so many policies of integration?

The concepts of acculturation, assimilation and integration have proved very persistent in migration studies, even though severely criticised. This may be because the scholarly concepts of integration and assimilation smoothly merged into policy language and became a discussion of nation-states' policy goals towards their immigrant populations?[2]

In Chicago sociology, assimilation was a type of interaction involving a thoroughgoing transformation of the individual personality through internalisation of values and norms. However, this quickly came to mean 'making someone different adjust to the norm' or simply Americanisation. This meaning persists in contemporary discussions, thus, assimilation is embedded in power relations between a majority demanding minorities to assimilate. This hierarchy is hidden behind a claimed concern for the immigrants' well-being. If the immigrant fails to assimilate she suffers, but if she refuses to take part in assimilation programmes it is her own fault. Her suffering is caused by reluctance to change. In other words, assimilation gives the powerful a veneer of innocence and 'innocence makes for legitimacy' [*Schwartz, 1985: 132*]. The concept of integration, on the other hand, denotes a mutual movement of two or more parties towards each other. Integration ideally mediates relations between immigrants, who are allowed to preserve their culture, and immigrant-receiving states, which promise equality between the immigrant minority and the dominant majority, although in reality rarely unconditional. Most studies which consider the host community as such at all, do so from the point of view of the effect on 'the host economy, political system, immigration laws and policies, and attitudes of its members on the adjustment of migrants, rather than on adaptation being made by members of the host community' [*Graves and Graves, 1974: 141*]. In a critical essay on the representation of immigrants, Schwartz further questions the integration paradigm on this basis. Irrespective of the conceptual distinction between assimilation and integration, success or failure to integrate are what researchers study, at least what research councils actually sponsor (indicated by the fact that cultures most resistant to integration are the most likely to be studied). Only by substituting 'integration' with 'identity', 'subjective identity formation', and 'cultural production' can we recover a critical research perspective [*Schwartz, 1990: 49*]. We still lack, however, adequate concepts for bringing *the migrant* and the complexity of *migrant experiences* into migration studies.

FROM TRADITION TO TRANSNATIONALISM

The world can no longer, if ever, be understood as international in the sense of being made up of independent, separate nations with solid boundaries. Instead it has become a transnational, inter-dependent system where national borders are increasingly permeable.[3] Capital, consumer goods, cultural ideas and migrants are globalised to an extent where any mapping of origin and belonging must be substituted by a mapping of social relations beyond boundaries. Crossing boundaries implies a crossing of mental or moral boundaries as much as geographic borders. The various social relations and multiple experiences of individual Dominican migrants demand that we break loose from our 'root' metaphors of society and culture as systems of bounded and articulated parts [*Barth, 1993: 4*]. People may live in several locations and/or take part in networks that transcend boundaries, and this will influence their daily lives and practices. In the age of transnationalism new forms of social relations are created, currently conceptualised as 'contextualised identities' [*Bachu, 1993*], 'transnational ethnicities' [*Kearney, 1991*], 'binational families' [*Chavez, 1988*], 'international families' [*Ho, 1993*], and 'transnational families' [*Wiltshire, 1992*]. These social relations all contain gendered dynamics.

When one rejects traditional approaches to migration and focuses instead on the lived experience of migration, cultural meeting places, and the generation of transnational lives, meanings and identities, then one must also reject the various models put forward earlier about forms of cultural integration. Neither the 'melting pot' model of cultural assimilation (presented in cultural theories of the world as existing of different, distinct cultures) nor the 'salad bowl' model of cultural pluralism (also called the cultural mosaic) can be accepted as appropriate conceptual tools any longer. Ideas of assimilation, integration, fusion or pluralism and the related metaphors of either melting pots or pressure cookers, mosaics or powder kegs, cannot grasp the cultural complexity of migration processes (though these metaphors may disclose important global power structures and specific local gender relations).

As suggested by Gupta and Ferguson [*1992: 16*] we need to turn 'from a project of juxtaposing pre-existing differences to one of exploring the construction of difference in historical process', and, as Vron Ware [*1992*] has suggested with reference to the intersections of race and gender, we need to move away from 'obsession with difference' towards 'relational connectedness' of the different identities. In the Dominican case this project includes, on the one hand, an analysis of colonialism as well as contemporary US political, economic and cultural domination of the home region and, on the other hand, an unpacking of the multiple layers of time, space and place-making in the cultural construction of Dominican identities. Thus, rapidly increasing global interdependence demands analytical concepts and theories capable of penetrating our former notions of neatly bounded and homogeneous entities. Although our analyses must be global in scale, specific localities do not lose their importance. Such places may receive even greater significance for their inhabitants because they are no longer viewed as natural conditions of life but, rather, as places invested with cultural significance as local communities carved out of hierarchically organised space [*Gupta and Ferguson, 1992*]. We must extend our analyses to include more than a single community study, but without losing a local perspective [*Barth, 1993: 30*]. How then do we proceed?

Recent theories of transnational migration are beginning to explore the complexity of economic, political, cultural, and personal relations. Although these theories emphasise various aspects of transnational processes, they all focus upon social relations and, thereby, bring several societies into a single ethnographic field.[4] These theories are helpful in that they open the way to explore the complexities of political, cultural and personal relations. Gender can now be treated in a much more serious way.

GENDER IDENTITY AND CULTURAL CHANGE

In her novel *How the Garcia Girls Lost Their Accents*, Dominican writer Julia Alvarez tells the story of four Dominican girls transplanted from the Dominican republic to New York City as a result of their parents' migration. In this chronicle of a family in exile,[5] the cultural differences of two nations are described through the eyes of the four daughters. New York is foreign and mysterious: laundromat, cornflakes, subway, snow. During the girls' teenage years the Dominican Republic becomes 'old hat': hair and nails, chaperones, itchy boys with all their macho strutting, unbuttoned shirts, hairy chests with gold chains and teensy gold crucifixes, a whole island of family.

The novel is the story of the clash between worlds. The incompatability of being an emancipated young woman from New York in the Dominican republic and the hardships and losses of being a Dominican woman in New York City are represented by the girls' presence on analysts' couches and in divorce courts. Back 'home' on a holiday visit one of the sisters considers that return would be the solution to her *split* identity:

> There has been too many stops on the road of the last twenty-nine years since her family left this island behind. She and her sisters have led so turbulent lives - so many husbands, homes, jobs, wrong turns among them. But look at her cousins, women with household and authority in their voices. Let this turn out to be my home, Yolanda wishes [*Alvarez, 1991: 11*].

The story of the Garcia girls is a mixture of fiction and autobiography, since the writer is partly relating her own experience as a first generation migrant. Moreover, it is about an earlier phase of Dominican migration before migration accelerated to contemporary levels. Although Dominican migrants still suffer many hardships, New York is not so foreign anymore. It has become another distant province of the Dominican Republic, since so many Dominicans now reside there and travel back and forth.

An interesting aspect of Alvarez's novel is that ethnic confusion finds expression in a split in gender identity. The most glaring cultural difference the Garcia girls must confront and handle is the contrast between machismo and the more egalitarian gender relations in New York City.

During fieldwork on the Upper West side of Manhattan I have found that while Dominican migrants live in two worlds, the women do not necessarily appear to suffer from the same confusion of identity as the Garcia girls did. Men, in contrast, seem to face many more difficulties as a result of the conflicting demands embedded in the Dominican concept of machismo.

Concepts shared and understood by people take on different meanings under migration. What machismo or being 'macho' entails depends on which side of the border you come from, as Guilbault [1989] has pointed out with reference to the Mexican/Chicano experience in the United States. She claims that the word 'macho' in an Hispanic context is primarily understood as meaning responsible, hardworking, a man in charge, a man who expresses strength through silence. But in the US, 'macho' is defined as a brutish, uncouth, selfish, loud, abrasive, capable of inflicting pain, and sexually promiscuous. So, while macho ennobles Latin males in Spanish, it devalues them in English. Moreover, she sees that this pattern is reflected in the conflicts which ethnic minority males generally experience in the US.

According to Guilbault, different interpretations of the term 'macho' arose on account of the feminist movement of the early 1970s. 'Suddenly a word that represented something positive in one culture became a negative prototype in another'[ibid.: 17].

However, 'macho' was never a univocal concept; it always possessed ambiguous connotations. The conflicting images of man-the-provider and man-the-sexual exploiter were then, and still are, constantly challenged in the Dominican Republic. Moreover, one problem with conceptualisations like honour and shame and the cultural construction of gender relations under overarching systems of machismo has been that we are left with no resources 'with which we might attempt to discern differences in interpretation of these values amongst parties differently situated' [Coombe, 1990: 224]. Therefore, migration and the meeting or clash between different cultures cannot be seen as the only condition under which the concept of 'macho' takes on different meanings. The ambiguity was already there. In other words, migration emphasises different aspects of the male identity that is expressed through different forms of male behaviour.

Not only does the dominant opinion in the United States challenge the meaning of 'macho', Dominicans living there do so as well. A Dominican family man in New York is expected to act macho, that is, be responsible, in a different way from when in the Dominican Republic. If he fails he will face sanctions from his own community. An illustrative example can be found in the case of the Suarez family,[6] who have lived in New York for nearly 15 years.

DOMINICAN MACHISMO

Orlando Suarez was considered a good family man when he first went to New York. Although he had broken with his first family (wife and daughter) in order to remarry Mercedes before he left the Republic, his own family (siblings) considered him responsible and behaving in a positive macho manner. After a few years in New York Mercedes decided to follow him, leaving their two children with her mother, but *she* soon realised their stay would not be as temporary as Orlando had continuously claimed and she sent for the children. After a few more years in New York, a third child was born, and the daughter from Orlando's first marriage also came to join the family. They were still a harmonious family, according to both family members and neighbours.

When their youngest child was seven years old, Orlando took up with another woman with whom he had yet another child. This time, however, his macho behaviour, that is, the proof of his sexual capacity, was negatively sanctioned. His own siblings, most of whom now lived in New York, came down on the side of his wife. What kind of a man was he to let down the family he brought to this foreign country? What kind of a man was he to leave a Dominican wife for a Puerto Rican *puta*?[6] Was he a man at all?

His wife interpreted his behaviour as macho in the following way:

> In my culture the man is 'el macho'. And my husband is macho as well. That means that he can do anything, anything without exception. Men can do anything, and women are left with no way of protesting, because men believe they can do anything. My man has another woman, but I cannot have another man. I don't want to suffer because I am a woman. I don't want to cry, because I am a woman. I have needs too. We are caught in this. Mentally caught. I am still young. I could remarry and have a better life. But next time it won't be with a Latino. Latino men are *machistas*.

Orlando's grown up daughters both threw him over, one of them referring to the *changed* macho behaviour of the father: 'I used to think that people never changed - no matter what, even though someone really needed to. But he became a total different person. He used to be a responsible father. But now! I don't love him anymore. I have told him, and I don't want to see him again.' The other daughter went so far as to challenge his manhood. To her, he was neither the husband of her mother nor her father. Whenever his name was mentioned in the family she refused to call him anything but *the dog*. If she visited her mother while he was in the house, she left immediately commenting that she did not want to be in a dog's house. If Orlando entered the house while she was already there, she would leave for the same reasons. Orlando was unable to use his paternal authority to stop her from leaving.

Surrounded by criticism and dislike, Orlando told family members and neighbours that he was not in love with his new woman. The only reason he stayed with her was because he felt *responsible* for their child. He, therefore, tried to refer to the positive values associated with manhood in order to regain respectability. But he never succeeded, since his wife, his older children and his siblings all responded with the argument that he could bring his illegitimate offspring with him, and continue to lead a proper family life with his 'real' family. His wife even offered to adopt his *bastardo* and treat him as if he were her own.

When Orlando could no longer take the loss of honour and *respeto* in the eyes of his family, he asked his wife, 'how do you expect me to stay in your house when you treat me as a dog? You don't even cook for me.' Mercedes responded, 'I'll cook for a dog. But how can I cook for someone who doesn't give me money for food?'

This reflected a central dilemma of machismo. Orlando had acted machista by taking another woman but simultaneously he had failed other obligations of macho behaviour by not providing for his family. The problems of the Suarez family suggests an ambiguity in the way the macho concept is used, as well as some change in emphasis on different aspects of machismo which came into play as a result of migration.

Changes in concepts of manhood have also been found in a study of Dominican drinking patterns in a small community in New England [*Gordon, 1978*]. Although an increased reliance on alcohol and excessive drinking have frequently been reported for migrants of minority group status residing in urban areas, Gordon found that Dominicans in this area, independent of age, occupation and background, had a lower alcohol consumption than Dominicans back on the island. Not only had the level of consumption decreased, but drinking took place only at weekends, it was 'calmer' and rarely led to fights. Moreover, alcohol consumption was far less closely associated with a macho image. Instead the macho ideal was being replaced by a different ideal of *el hombre serio*, the serious man who proves himself by hard work, sacrifice and dedication to the family. According to Gordon [*1978: 65*], 'this image markedly contrasts with the macho role of the padre de familia in the Dominican Republic who, although he provides for his family, also proves his manliness by heavy drinking, carousing, and fighting to protect his honor'.

Migration only indirectly creates new ideals of manhood. There are many contributory factors. New roles and expectations for wives together with the migrant ideology to economise, progress and to sacrifice has created *el hombre serio*. New and better job opportunities for women have led to women's increased authority and independence, an independence that readily leads to divorce if the husband fails 'to show dedication to home and heart', Gordon concludes.

FEMALE INDEPENDENCE

Pessar [*1987a; 1987b*] has argued that Dominican women's status as wage workers has improved their position in the household and has modified their orientation to an eventual return to the Dominican Republic. 'Because wage work has brought immigrant women many personal gains, including greater household authority and self-esteem, they are much more active agents than men in prolonging the households' stay in the United States' [*Pessar, 1987a: 123*].

That wage work experience should be the determining factor for greater female independence is somehow contrasted by the fact, and here I quote Pessar, 'that the international migrant stream is comprised predominantly of middle class urban men and women *who were employed prior to migration*' [*Pessar, 1982*] (my italics). The great majority of Dominican women I met during fieldwork in Washington Heights and who left the Dominican Republic as adults (including Mercedes) had also been employed prior to migration. Therefore, the increased female independence and changing ideals of manhood from *macho* to *hombre serio* cannot be said to derive solely from female participation in wage work. The old argument of Marxist feminism that equality in the labour market automatically leads to domestic social equality, has been uncritically adopted by both Pessar and Gordon. Such a simple connection remains in doubt.

Sutton argues that Caribbean migrants represent a transnationalisation of identities as well as an *internationalisation* of gender.[8] The gender dimensions of transmitting ethnicity and race articulate with the equally gendered meanings associated with 'public' and 'private' spheres of life. Here ethnicity is located in the private sphere, race in the public. Her argument is embedded in an analysis of the old, European, female immigrant compared to the African American population in the United States, as well as of the new experiences of both Latino and Caribbean women in the new migration stream. Her analysis suggests how ethnicity is inherited differently by men and women, and more important it shows that the images and ideologies surrounding women as reproducers vary according to the different status of women in different cultures.

In the existing literature Dominican women are represented as subordinated members of a patriarchal culture, see Pessar [*1987b*]; Georges [*1990*]; Grasmuck and Pessar [*1991*]; and Sutton [*1992*]. Patriarchal family traditions are taken to imply that men as heads of households are the persons around which migration exchanges occur. Moreover, Dominican machismo is interpreted solely in the 'Mediterranean' sense. Since Dominican gender relations have been described as diverging from the Hispanic pattern, economy more than culture has been given explanatory force. The Dominican multiple mate form, characterised by unstable marital unions, high illegitimacy rates, male marginality within the household, high instances of matrifocal or female-headed households, has been seen as a coping strategy for women in the lower economic sectors [cf. *Brown, 1973*], not as a cultural practice in its own right. Hence, creolised or Afro-Caribbean cultural elements have been more or less erased from the Dominican cultural picture.[9] Whereas we are informed about the *absence* of a male provider, attention is seldom given to the presence of bonds between siblings, female bonds between mothers and daughters: women as providers. If we turn the Suarez chronicle opposite down, a strong solidarity between women is revealed. Mercedes, her own daughter, and even Orlando's daughter from his first marriage all view Orlando's behaviour as unacceptable. During my stay with the Suarez family, Mercedes was in the process of claiming her mother under the family reunification programme.

Therefore, the view presented by the majority of observers of the Dominican migration process is far too simple because, first, Dominican women actually migrate on their own to a large extent, and, secondly, they, as well as their West Indian sisters, act as cultural brokers in numerous situations.

From fieldwork experience with both Dominican men and women in New York, I am convinced that ethnicity and gender and the interrelationship between these identities cannot be studied without also including class. (And this, of course, complicates the study of ethnicity still further.) In the Dominican case, men more often initiate the migration process in middle class families, whereas more female-initiated migration is seen in the lower classes.

Men from the middle classes blame the American welfare system, as well as Dominican women, for the hardships faced by Dominican families in New York. Since women are no longer dependent on men for financial support they become independent and seek divorce. While this is a statement of a real problem, it is also blames Dominican women for losing their ethnicity, for no longer maintaining their role as the backbone in the Dominican family.

Women also blame the welfare system, but on the grounds that it enables men to have more than one wife at the same time, since the state helps support the mothers and their kids. Ironically, the possibilities for 'negative' machista behaviour, showing great sexual capacity by having more women, are enlarged in the foreign cultural setting, and not seen as embedded in Dominican 'backwardness'. Here I agree with Marita Eastmond [*1993: 36*] who suggests that continuity does not mean an absence of change but rather the ability to integrate change in culturally meaningful ways. The above-mentioned perceptions of the American welfare system may not reveal the policy intentions of the system, but they do indeed reveal how this system is perceived, and perceived differently, by Dominicans with various cultural backgrounds and differently situated in the power structure. Seen in this perspective, Dominican interpretations certainly make sense! It also suggests that assumptions that Western ideologies of egalitarian gender relations necessarily lead to more egalitarian relationships in migrant populations must be treated with caution [*Buijs, 1993: 5*].

So while it seems obvious that ethnicity is experienced differently by women and men, it seems as obvious that the different experiences are embedded in the different ways ethnic identity relates to images and ideologies surrounding women within different social classes. These gender and class-specific ethnic ideologies are mainly communicated through changes in gender identity. The female counterpart to *el hombre serio* is the capable woman, *la mujer con capacidad*. Lower class males do not blame divorce and loss of ethnicity on women. 'Women change faster. They integrate more easily. They have more ability'.[10]

The internationalisation of gender through the feminist movement has perhaps given rise to a greater acknowledgement of female *strength*. Among Dominicans I believe that the 'capable women', more than the negative prototype of macho [*Guilbault, 1989*], has been an important outcome of this movement. Both manhood and womanhood are ambiguous concepts with 'good' as well as 'bad' qualities. Transnational migration *and* the simultaneous process of modernisation in the Dominican Republic have contributed to this change.

EPILOGUE

An ironic but unfortunate indication of changed gender relations can be deduced from a common response to, and interpretation of, the public information campaign on AIDS. The Dominican campaign has followed international patterns and drawn attention to the increased risk of infection from promiscuity or frequent changes of partners. During fieldwork in the Dominican Republic I heard more than a few men discussing the issue by stating that AIDS was not a 'real' sickness, but something the government had made up to keep men from having more women in order to protect the family, and that the government was involved in a conspiratorial plot with local women and women's organisations. Besides misreading important public information, such interpretations show *both* the stubbornness of machismo *and* the male acknowledgement of changes in power relations between women and men. Interestingly women and the state are seen as having mutual interests in controlling *male* sexual behaviour. Men, whose personal power lay in sexuality and family, and who were understood to be the source of patriarchal state power, are actually complaining that women and the state form a coalition. This contradicts the assumptions of the honour/shame complex, which see men's control over female sexuality as the most important basic element, as well as much feminist writing on patriarchy. If this complaint has any basis, then a revision of the feminist critique of the state is in order.

NOTES

1. Rosaldo's statement only holds 'true' for western-type modern nation states. In 'cultural' nation-states, for example, Bhutan, preserving traditional culture and renouncing western ways may be an absolute condition for obtaining state employment and are the moral imperatives to being a proper citizen.
2. For a discussion of a similar process of co-optation between development theory and development policy, see Wilson [1992].
3. The extent to which national boundaries are permeable to different classes of people vary. Or, perhaps more precisely, the conditions under which different classes of people enter a foreign nation state vary. As we saw in the case of Haitian boat refugees in summer 1994, the global, transnational world is denied the poor.
4. For a transnational perspective on migration, see Sutton [1987], Kearney [1991], and Glick-Schiller et al. [1992].
5. Although almost exclusively described as a traditional labour migrant population, Dominican migrants in New York also consist of a notable group of political exiles. The latter mainly left the island in the turbulent years following the overthrow of the Dominican dictator, Trujillo, in 1961.
6. The 'Suarez' family, as well as the given names, are pseudonyms.
7. Puerto Rican whore. The fact that some Dominican women call Puerto Rican women whores does not mean that they actually are whores, but they may represent a threat. Puerto Rican women are US citizens, and therefore very 'attractive'. Marrying a Puerto Rican has been a common way to legalise the migrant status for many Dominicans, often as a *matrimonio de negocio*, marriage of convenience.
8. I have been very inspired by Connie Sutton. Her thoughts about transnationalisation of identities and internationalisation of gender are set out in a working draft paper she gave me and in discussions in her kitchen during my fieldwork in New York.
9. For an analysis of the creolisation of Dominican culture, see Sørensen [1993].
10. Male cleaner, Washington Heights, 1991.

REFERENCES

Alvarez, Julia, 1991, *How the Garcia Girls Lost Their Accents*, New York: Algonquin Books of Chapel Hill.
Archer, Margaret S., 1985, 'The Myth of Cultural Integration, *The British Journal of Sociology*, Vol.35, No.3, pp.333–53.
Bachu, Parminder, 1993, 'Identities Constructed and Reconstructed: Representations of Asian Women in Britain', in Buijs (ed.) [1993].
Barth, Fredrik, 1993, *Balinese Worlds*, Chicago, IL: University of Chicago Press.
Borneman, John, 1986, 'Emigres as Bullets/Immigration as Penetration. Perceptions of the Marielitos', *The Journal of Popular Culture*, Vol.20, No 3, pp.73–92.
Brown, Susan, 1973, 'Lower Economic Sector Female Mating Patterns in the Dominican Republic: A Comparative Analysis', in Ruby Rohrlich-Leavitt (ed.), *Women Cross-Culturally: Change and Challenge*, The Hague and Paris: Mouton Publishers.
Buijs, Gina, 1993, 'Introduction', in Gina Buijs (ed.), *Migrant Women: Crossing Boundaries and*

Changing Identities, Oxford & Providence, RI: Berg Publishers.

Carnegie, Charles V., 1987, 'A Social Psychology of Caribbean Migrations: Strategic Flexibility in the West Indies', in Barry B. Levine (ed.), *The Caribbean Exodus*, New York: Praeger.

Chavez, Leo R., 1988, 'Settlers and Sojourners: The Case of Mexicans in the United States', *Human Organization*, Vol.47, No.2, pp.95-108.

Coombe, Rosemary J., 1990, 'Barren Ground: Re-conceiving Honour and Shame in the Field of Mediterranean Ethnography', *Anthropologica*, Vol. XXXII, pp.221–38.

Eastmond, Marita, 1993, 'Reconstructing Life: Chilean Refugee Women and the Dilemmas of Exile', in Buijs (ed.) [*1993*].

Georges, Eugenia, 1990, *The Making of a Transnational Community: Migration Development and Cultural Change in the Dominican Republic*, New York: Columbia University Press.

Gilmore, David D., 1990, *Manhood in the Making: Cultural Concepts of Masculinity*, New Haven, CT and London: Yale University Press.

Glick-Schiller, Nina, Basch, Linda, and Cristina Blanc-Szanton (eds.), 1992, *Towards a Transnational Perspective on Migration: Race, Class, Ethnicity, and Nationalism Reconsidered*, New York: New York Academy of Sciences.

Gordon, Andrew J., 1978, 'Hispanic Drinking after Migration: the Case of Dominicans', *Medical Anthropology*, Fall, pp.61–84.

Grasmuck, Sherri, and P.R. Pessar, 1991, *Between two Islands - Dominican International Migration*, Berkeley, Los Angeles, CA and New York: University of California Press.

Graves, Nancy B. and Theodore D. Graves, 1974, 'Adaptive Strategies in Urban Migration', *Annual Review of Anthropology*, No.3, pp.117–51.

Guilbault, Rose del Castillo, 1989, 'Untranslateable worlds: Macho', *Mesoamerica*, Vol.2, No.2, pp.16–17.

Gupta, Akhil and James Ferguson, 1992, 'Beyond "Culture": Space, Identity, and the Politics of Difference', *Cultural Anthropology*, Vol.7, No.1, pp.6–23.

Ho, Christine G.T., 1993, 'The Internationalization of Kinship and the Feminization of Caribbean Migration: The Case of Afro-Trinidadian Immigrants in Los Angeles', *Human Organization*, Vol.52, No.1, pp.32–40.

Kearney, Michael, 1991, 'Borders and Boundaries of State and Self at the End of Empire', *Journal of Historical Sociology*, Vol.4, No.1, pp.52–74.

Malkki, Liisa, 1992, 'National Geographic: The Rooting of Peoples and the Territorialization of National Identity Among Scholars and Refugees', *Cultural Anthropology*, Vol.7, No.1, pp.24–44.

Morokvasic, Mirjana, 1984, 'Birds of Passage are also Women', *International Migration Review*, Vol.18, No.4, pp.886–906.

Pessar, Patricia, 1982, 'Kinship Relations of the Production in the Migration Process: The Case of Dominican Migration to the United States', *Occasional Paper No.32*, New York: New York University, Center for Latin American and Caribbean Studies.

Pessar, Patricia, 1987a, 'The Dominicans: Women in the Household and the Garment Industry', in Nancie Foner (ed.), *New Immigrants in New York*, New York: Columbia University Press.

Pessar, Patricia, 1987b, 'The Linkage between the Household and Workplace of Dominican Women in the United States', in C. Sutton and E. Chaney (eds.), *Caribbean Life in New York City: Sociocultural Dimensions*, New York: Center for Migration Studies.

Rosaldo, Renato, 1989, *Culture and Truth: The Remaking of Social Analysis*, Boston, MA: Beacon Press.

Schwartz, Jonathan M., 1985, *Reluctant Hosts: Denmark's Reception of Guest Workers*, Kultursociologiske Skrifter No.21, Copenhagen: Akademisk Forlag.

Schwartz, Jonathan M., 1990, 'On the Representation of Immigrants in Denmark', in Flemming Røgilds (ed.), *Every Cloud has a Silver Lining*, Studies in Cultural Sociology No.28, Copenhagen: Akademisk Forlag.

Sørensen, Ninna Nyberg, 1991, 'Westside Story 1991', *Dansk Sociologi*, Vol.4, No.2, pp.108–117.

Sørensen, Ninna Nyberg, 1993, 'Creole Culture, Dominican Identity', *Folk*, Vol.35, pp.17–35.

Stepputat, Finn, 1992, *Beyond Relief: Life in a Guatemalan Refugee Settlement in Mexico*, Copenhagen: Institute of Cultural Sociology.

Sutton, Constance R., 1987, 'The Caribbeanization of New York City and the Emergence of a Transnational Socio-cultural System', in C.R. Sutton and E. Chaney (eds.), op. cit.

Sutton, Constance R., 1992, 'Transnational Identities and Cultures: Caribbean Immigrants in the United States', in Michael D'Innocezno and Joseph P. Sierefman, *Immigration and Ethnicity: American Society*, 'Melting Pot' or 'Salad Bowl'?, New York: Greenwood Press.

Ware, Vron, 1992, *Beyond the Pale: White Women, Racism and History*, London & York: New Verso.

Wilson, Fiona, 1992, 'Faust: The Developer', *CDR Working Paper 92:5*, Copenhagen: Centre for Development Research.

Wiltshire, Rosina, 1992, 'Implications of Transnational Migration for Nationalism: The Caribbean Example', in Glick-Shiller *et al.* [*1992*].